Betwixt 2
Shores

To Pauline Atkins
Many Thanks.
Gary 24/9/2023

William Henry

Acknowledgement

I express my deepest appreciation to Her Excellency Karen May Hill, High Commissioner, Antigua and Barbuda. In addition, I want to thank my friend and former colleague Liz and Terry Boley, who first encouraged me forty-two years ago to write Betwixt 2 Shores, for their support and guidance in creating the book.

Sincere appreciation to Jehu Henry, Sandra Hibbert, Stacey Shelley, Wayne James (aka Rample), Phillip Ramsey (aka Vaden), Marc Jackson, Yvette Longmoore, Lionel O'Brien, Dr Coleen M. James, Ashanti Paris, Leslie Garshong, Beatrice Williams, Stephen Dore, and Anthony Browne (aka Chowie). **Kemarl Michael Nathaniel Fontilio.** Ron Sewell, Peter Denis and Shyam Seegobin.

For those family and friends that are not mentioned, you are very much loved, and I thank you all.

Foreword

"Windrush" was not all nice and rosy. It is hoped that silenced voices will be unlocked. I was moved to recount the traumas I have endured because there is no substantive understanding of the damages resulting from the "Windrush" scandal on descendants' lives.

The announcement for rebuilding the "Motherland" following the Second World War shattered my world. I spent years not knowing my biological parents because they answered the "call". Subsequently, I was removed from my homeland and taken to the "Motherland", and within less than a year of being in the "Motherland", I was classified as "maladjusted" by the same system that enslaved my African ancestors, colonised my homeland and caused separation and denial of family life. The traumas that I experienced were endless.

Unfortunately, the "Windrush" generation's descendants remain the targets of a hostile environment, racism, exclusion, separation, abandonment, exploitation, violence, murder, and injustices. The Windrush scandal was influenced by the impact of Empires and

Colonialisation that separated established civilisations and original settlers from their communities.

Terminologies

Baderation	Botheration
Benna	Secular Music
Can cup	Enamel Cup
Calypso	Caribbean Music Genre
Coal pot	Cooking Stove
Chop Up	Combination of vegetables used for breakfast
Cut ass	Flogging
Dust Up	Fighting
Gaulins	Egrets
Golliwog	Non-White Person
Grip	Suitcase
Ground provision:	Root Vegetables (Dasheen, Yam, Sweet Potato, Cassava, eddo. The list is not exhausted).
J'ouvert	Day Break
Jumbie	Ghost
Jack	Plastic Bucket-Shower Replacement
Latrine	Outdoor Toilet

Lawd, ah wah kine ah el mi deh inna? Lord, what is this hell I am in?

Lucian Jamboree:	Social gathering
Negro Ground	Farming Allotments

Pan	Water Pond
Patois	Caribbean-based Creole Language
Pickney	Child/Children
Poe	Commode Bucket with lid
Road Hogs	Reckless Driver
Saga Boy	A well-groomed Caribbean male
Sambo	A derogatory term used to define a person of African background
Sloshed	Drunk Driver
Souse	Pickled pig's meat served with clear broth
White Gold	Cane Sugar
Yabba	Cooking utensils Replacement

Table of Contents

Chapter 1

Place of Birth

I was born in New Winthropes Village, Antigua, in 1960. My father left my mother whilst she was seven months pregnant with me to "Answer the Call" to rebuild the UK following the Second World War. Subsequently, after my birth in August 1960, my mother left Antigua to join my father in the "Motherland" and help rebuild the UK. I was left with my maternal grandmother at the age of seven months.

My maternal grandmother, sisters, and extended family members primarily raised me. I was the youngest of four siblings born in Antigua and the only male. My family (maternal grandmother Mary Henry, (aka Mem), my sisters, nannies, Mama Juliette, and Harty were all very important to me; they were all I knew and had.

My family was always present for me. In retrospect, I was very well cared for; the way I was nurtured and socialised, I would not trade for anything. I was ten when I first met my biological parents; throughout my primary age, I never received a phone call, any letter or postcard from my parents. Due to the "answering the call" with rebuilding the "Motherland," I suffered the loss of never bonding with my parents.

As a child growing up in Antigua, I had to respect my household and my community. There were rules with clear boundaries that dictated how I should behave and compose myself. For instance, if an elder visited my grandmother, I would greet the elder and disappear from their presence, as it would be considered rude to remain in their company. I was raised to respect my elders, which included teachers.

Education was paramount in the Antiguan culture; it encouraged young people to do well in school. Antiguan parents saw education as the way forward for unlocking talents and preparing young people for the world of work. We afforded teachers the same level of respect as we would to our parents. I have never known who set those rules, but they were set to be followed; they were not one-off decrees but lifelong. Maybe some were created from conception and handed down from birth to the grave.

NewWinthropes is held very close to my heart; I am very proud of where I come from and the treasured methods of nurturing and socialising. Households differ considerably. Some households were ok with playing secular music, young boys used expletives, which were reserved for an adult male, discipline was not rigid and strict, some young people did not have chores, and some got a penny a week for doing chores.

In the village, some older adults were entrusted by parents to look after their children. They would also help by collecting clothes from the line before it rained and keeping an eye on the pot on the fire until the parent returned from town. Those bygone days gave true meaning to the adage, "It takes a village to bring up a child." The idea of employing a nanny as we know it today was unimaginable and unforthcoming except for a lucky few. A neighbour was not just the person who lived across the street but a person if you were short of cooking oil, sugar and salt that could be asked, which was the norm in old NewWinthropes.

Most children in Antigua come from restricted socioeconomic backgrounds, income, education, employment, community safety, and social support. All of these factors dictate the socialisation process. It may seem like many challenges, but the experience created an unbroken spirit that strives to do well in me. Most young people from NewWinthropes are raised in sole-parent households where women head the household. Notwithstanding the lack of male presence, the sole female household has produced some very good quality young people, including chief medical officers, nurses, engineers, lawyers, and educators; the list is not exhaustive.

Ancestral Home

My ancestral family home is on a hill, which was, back then, the highest habitational point within the village. I have fond memories of my childhood growing up in NewWinthropes. My siblings and I had daily chores such as cleaning the house in the mornings and preparing breakfast and laundry. Weekly pocket money was unheard of in my family home. We all had chores and got on sweeping the yard, feeding chickens and going to the hills to gather firewood. My efforts were insignificant compared to my siblings, as I was too young to make a difference. All of the daily duties had to be completed before going to school. Therefore, our day would start at 6 AM.

Our house was made out of pitch pine wood, comprising two bedrooms, a living room, an outside kitchen, a bathroom, planks for the pillows, galvanised sheets for the roof and sides, and the same with the outdoor toilet, (latrine), a prominent pit hole. An elevated seat was made from board and cut to the size of the pit. I never liked using the pit for the fear that I might fall in; the stench was unwelcoming. Instead, I opted for the mobile night-time toilet, the Poe, where I only had contend with my smell and no fear of falling in. We never had electricity.

We relied on hurricane lamps and kerosene; surprisingly, the bright, dazzling, glowing light was sufficient for our purpose.

We did not have direct running water, so water had to be carried from the village to the hill, assuming the main water supply was not turned off. Water shortage was a standard feature in the village. We could go several weeks without having access to fresh water. If the main water supply were turned off, we would have to walk miles to the nearest pan (pond) to get water. The roof of the house was covered with galvanised sheets, and the sidings had to gutter all around the building with spouts, one at the front side, middle and back.

The rain spouts were connected to iron drums at each section to gather rainwater during a heavy downpour. The drums were treated to prevent mosquitoes from breeding at the bottom of the drums, and each drum was covered with stainless mesh. Heavy rain was a respite for the water carriers, as the rain would fill the drums. We didn't rely on weather metrology to forecast the weather, e.g., expected rainfall was determined by the cloud's intensity and the sky's darkness.

Watching the sky rolling like a monster gathering rapid momentum was intriguing. Suddenly rain drops beat like a drum on the galvanised roof before the entire earth was saturated, the water drums being filled without any significant effort, and the rolling sky monster would unleash flashes of lightning followed by rolling thunder simultaneously.

I knew from an early age that my village was unique; there was a captivating special feeling within the village. The overall feeling derives from uncontaminated air, thriving wildlife, mongoose, various species of birds, ducks and multi-coloured butterflies, and a scenic view where land and sea make beauty. Cloudless blue sky, brilliant, piercing diamond sunshine on my skin, it was impossible to be unhappy. As I stepped out from my family house, I was surrounded by blooming trees of coconut, tamarind, papaya, dumps, genips, soursop, sugar apple, pomegranate, banana, breadfruit, an abundance of fruit trees, leaving me spoilt for choice for breakfast and lunch.

Despite the evidence of the abundance of mouth-watering fruits, my day could only start with a cup of Lipton tea or bush tea. My grandmother was a firm believer in the value of bush tea. Therefore, Lipton was only sometimes an option. I preferred bush tea, but it depends on the bush type, as they are some very bitter bushes, and some were very tasty such as fresh eucalyptus tea and Nunu Balsam which was my favourite. These teas were packed with exciting flavours.

My tea was served in a can cup, which always seemed to keep the tea hotter than necessary, mainly when my mind was preoccupied with climbing a fruit tree. I remain an avid tea drinker. My day must start with a cup of tea; I drink Early Grey or bush tea, mainly bush tea, which I either travel with from Antigua or purchase from a supplier in London.

Middle Passage

"Middle Passage" refers to the route to convey West Africans forcibly taken away from their native lands. and were taken directly to the Americas and the Caribbean involuntarily as indentured servants.

The Middle Passage followed three routes:

> **First route:** Europe to Africa
>
> **Second route:** Africa to America
>
> **Third route:** America to Europe.

Race divided slavery between Africans from European slavery. The Europeans established their ideas of what slavery meant to them and defined the category of people whom they considered enslavable people. Over twelve million people were captured and trafficked from the African Continent. Before the enslaved people were taken to ships destined for the "New World," they were stripped of their possessions and their hair was shaved. Ships were explicitly designed to traffic enslaved people for huge profits. One of the slave ships, the Zong, was used to traffic enslaved people from Ghana through the Americas to the Caribbean. The Zong first left Ghana in 1871 with approximately four hundred and fifty-five enslaved people destined through the Americas to the Caribbean.

The Middle Passage journey lasted approximately ninety days, subject to the weather condition. The enslaved men were permanently shackled, and the women and children were left unshackled.

The men and women were kept on separate decks. The conditions on the slave ships were horrendous. No toilets were available for the enslaved people, which caused them to remain in faeces and urine in an environment with limited ventilation throughout the inhumane journey.

The roof measurement where the enslaved people were housed was approximately four feet high, which made it difficult for them to stand. They were closely jammed together (almost spoon-like), a position they maintained for most of the journey. Disease spread throughout the decks among the crew members and the enslaved people. Sicknesses include malaria, yellow fever, smallpox, dysentery, influenza and measles. They endured temperatures over a hundred degrees and coped with traumatic episodes of people dying next to them. The trauma of this experience caused mental suffering, violent outburst, and disorientation. It is impossible to understand fully the trauma that the enslaved people went through of not knowing where they were being taken to and what the outcome would be for them. They were on an involuntary voyage void of understanding, anticipation, no meaning and complete helplessness.

The enslaved victims of the Middle Passage were treated less than humans, crammed on decks like sardines. They travelled across the Atlantic with only their religious persuasions that were different from their masters who had enslaved them; they were destined to foreign lands unknown to them. The conditions offered to the slaves were gruesome, grotesque, gnarled and beyond human comprehension of 'civilisation'. The slave ancestors could only have looked to their cultural norms and religions for their survival to endure their plight of being enslaved.

The trafficked enslaved people were given six to eight hours per day for "recreational" purposes where they were taken to the upper decks to entertain the crew members, while the male and female were kept separated. The recreational period was designed for crew members' pleasure. The women were raped and the men had to dance for the pleasure of crew members. However, there were attempts made by enslaved people to kill crew members and take charge of the boat. Unfortunately, their efforts were often aborted because they were in shackles and lack the necessary ammunition to make their nightmare become their reality.

The African culture is not limited to one religious belief and practice. Still, on the plantations, Christianity was the only acceptable religion, but the slaves were able to make faith meaningful outside the predominant religion of their 'masters' through singing, clapping of hands, drumming and dancing; they were able to commune in keeping with their African culture, and it was part of their mental emancipation. In many Caribbean islands, the slaves' religion remains part of worship.

My grandmother was a devout Christian; my sisters and I had to attend church every Sunday, and our church clothing could not be worn apart from going to church. Fornication, drinking, and smoking were forbidden. Immediately after the first crowing of the cock she would wake my sisters and me from our slumber and prepare for our weekly church attendance.

We rose and took our showers. I had four sisters. Each one usually takes ages in the shower. Being the only boy, I had no problem showering in the open air. They were variations in how they dressed, but most females wore pleated skirts, which gave the impression of elegance, femininity and styling of their hair. All of them had different coloured hair ribbons.

We were only excused from attending church because of sickness. We attended The Pilgrim Holiness Church, which has become The Wesleyan Holiness Church. For many of us, church attendance was a source of support. People listened without being judgemental but offered prayers as an alternative; attendees were encouraged to have 'faith in God.'

We had a light breakfast, which I think was a deliberate plot of our grandmother to avoid us sleeping in church. We attended the local branch church, and thirty minutes before the commencement of Sunday School, the church bell would toll by the bell ringer, alerting us that Sunday School was about to start. The bell was made from a thick piece of iron with a thin iron strip. Church attendance was a whole day event; I would arrive in church feeling sleepy.

I found it challenging to stay awake during the church service and looked forward to the extended prayer session where we would be on our knees. This gave me a chance to catch up on some much-needed sleep. However, some people would start snoring and drooling and their mothers would quickly wake them up with a firm tap. Despite this, I enjoyed attending church because I could hang out with my friends, although sometimes we slept.

I looked forward to the end of the service at 1 **PM** and to heading home for Sunday dinner, rice and peas, macaroni pie, coleslaw, green salad, stew chicken, stew fish or mutton, washed down with ginger beer, soursop, or homemade lemonade, dessert was subject to fruits that were in season. After Sunday's lunch, we would prepare to return to church for the extended Sunday School, which started at 3 PM -5 PM. The extended Sunday School was devoted to learning bible verses' and committing them to memory: For God so loved the world that he gave His only begotten son, John 3:16, you shall love your neighbour as yourself, Matthew 22:39. At the end of the lessons we were issued with a slip for the next week's lesson then we would be expected to pray until the commencement of revival service at 6 PM.

Many of us would sneak out to visit a local vendor and spend part of our church collection on candy. However, we never failed to collect the following week's memory verse and topic, as it was evident that we were in attendance. We would return in time for the commencement of the revival service at 6 PM, and we were always back in church on time. The service went on until 9 PM. The service would start with choruses, songs from songbooks, testimonies, sermons and altar calls. At the end of the year, young people were rewarded for their efforts to be in attendance for the year with a Christmas present.

I usually walked barefoot around our land, my village, as I liked the invigorating feeling of going without shoes regardless of it being concrete, dirt and grass. I liked the sensation of having my feet on the ground. I recall vividly the day when public workers came to pave the road, which ran directly outside my nanny's, Mama Juliet's house. I was four years old; I watched with interest as the workers paved the road from top to bottom. Immediately the workers completed their work and left for the day; I ran out into the wet cement, Mama Juliet scolded me, but my footprints remain fifty-eight years later. However, there was the exception when I had to wear shoes, such as attending church, school or town.

When I was two years old, I visited St. John's, a city in Antigua and Barbuda, with my fourth eldest sister and Mama Juliet. A professional photographer photographed my sister and me during our visit. However, the local Antiguan confectionery vendors were quite noticeable during our outing. The street market was also very colourful. Mama Juliet allowed my sister and me to choose a range of candy to bring back home.

St. John is a well-laid-out town, with its streets running parallel. The indigenous people of Antigua are primarily descendants of Ghana, West Africa. The street market allows vendors and buyers alike to gather to gossip and make their purchases. The scene was busy and lively. St. John is typical of most towns in the Caribbean; buildings are reminders of its colonial era, not for decorative effect.

The native people of Antigua are talented in creating beautiful handicrafts, including intricate beadwork that reflects their African roots. As tourism is popular on the island, there is a high demand for souvenirs for tourists.

The people of Antigua have been quick to meet this demand and have shown great creativity in their work. They use natural materials like shells and weave by hand to make valuable items such as hats, bags, and baskets. These products are popular among both locals and visitors.

Market Street St Johns Antigua

Street vendors and a customer going at it

Exchange between shopper and vendors

Generic fruits and vegetables

First visit to the town in 1962

Chapter 2

Pastimes

My sisters were easy to get along with, but they were constantly engaged in doing "girls" activities. However, my second eldest sister would not hesitate to ride a donkey or a horse bareback and keep firm control of either, similar to a boy. She would also play Marble and Warri. I saw myself as being inquisitive. I always sought adventure; the elders usually called me "baderation".

There was an unoccupied property at the back of our property. I later learned that that property was a mass burial ground of our slave ancestors. The property is overgrown with bushes, trees including fruit trees. It was my personal space; I would climb the tamarind tree to pick tamarind when they were in season. I gathered enough tamarind to make tamarind jam; my fourth eldest sister would join me in making the jam.

The jam was made in disused Milo tin over a log fire with bricks to support the tin container. Once the jam was cooked, we would feast on bread and jam. I was always armed with my homemade catapult, which I used to catch wood pigeons to roast. I shared my catch with our cats and dogs, who could always smell the roasting. My friends would visit, and we would engage in card games such as snap. The game was fun to play, but we tended to get loud. Card games were always played when my grandmother was not home, as it would be viewed as the 'devil's game.

I used to look forward to Friday evenings because it was a time when NewWinthropes came alive, the local bar played Calypso, people young and old interacted, and there was a happy family atmosphere. Local vendors could sell local confectionery, fudge, sugar cake, peppermint candy, coconut drops, guava cheese, tamarind balls, and of course, Ms B's churned ice cream and savoury products.

Apart from Ms B's churned ice cream delight, she specialised in making and selling black pudding. The term 'black pudding' is misleading because the product is not shaped or cooked as a pudding but as a big pipe-like sausage. Antiguans also refer to it as rice pudding. It was made from a pig's intestine, packed with various herbs, spices, rice, sweet potatoes and pig's blood. The black pudding was never a hit with me, but most participated by eating it with bread and souse; my preferred option was baked shellfish and bread.

A carefree lifestyle was pursued that enabled me to roam safely, independently and freely interact with others. There was no mod cons. Therefore, we had to be intuitive, creative and innovative in creating play materials for social pastimes or relying on activities passed on from elders. My favourite pastimes were marbles, steel pan, cricket and kite flying. We made our kites from coconut veins and newspaper.

Kite flying is a traditional pastime during Easter in remembrance of Christ's resurrection, but it is not limited to Easter per se. The first Monday in May is Antigua's Labour Day, a national holiday where all schools, colleges, universities and public offices are closed. All political parties and their supporters meet for rallies on specified streets in the city. After that, they converge at beaches for different party supporters. However, Antiguans do not need a public holiday to visit the beach or for a beach party.

Easter Monday Kite Flying in Antigua

Warri, Board games like Chess, draughts and chequered are well known worldwide, but Warri and its twelve seed-filled boards are lesser known - depending on where you're from. People from the West African sphere would recognise it at once. In Ghana, predominantly Among the Ashanti tribe, it is referred to as Oware, and it is always played with two people. Oware is reportedly the oldest game in the world, about fifteen thousand years old.

The game was brought to the Caribbean in the 17th Century. The slaves introduced their methods for playing the game. The game's purpose is to capture the house of the opposite opponent; the players need to be able to mentally calculate the moves necessary to capture the opponent's house. In Antigua and Barbuda, the game is called "Warri". Warri is a favourite pastime in most Caribbean Islands, but it is mainly played in Antigua and Barbuda; the game has its enthusiasts.

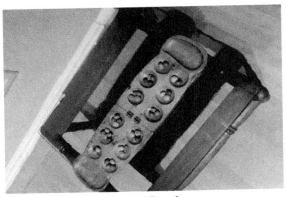

Warri Board

Steel pan instruments are made from disused oil drums; the pans are cut in varying depths. Some drums are shallow, and others are deep, depending on whether they were required to make bass or alto instruments. The steel pans were heated over a fire. After they have attained the required temperature, they are tempered with water and hammered into the required shape.

The bottom of the pan is marked off using chalk in several sectors. An experienced steel pan builder marks them out. The marked-out areas are punched and chiselled along each line of a pattern. Every band has distinctive colours and designs, painted uniformly on each instrument.

I never took part in creating the steelpan, but playing the steelpan was a favourite pastime, as I was allowed to play the instrument in tune with others. When instruments were ready, a cord was connected to the instrument to be borne over the shoulders and kept in place. Instruments were played with dexterity and accuracy and often from memory. The sound of music created from steel pan was pleasing to the ears.

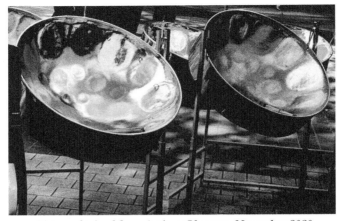

Picture obtained from Antigua Observer, November 2020

Calypso

Calypso is a musical genre that blends French Creole and carnival influences to create a jazzy rhythm. It has its roots in the slaves brought to work on sugar plantations in Trinidad and other Caribbean islands. These slaves were forbidden from communicating with one another, so they used Calypso to communicate and mock their slave masters covertly. Early Calypsonians sang in French Patois, and the music was led by a prominent figure who helped unite the slaves through their music.

Caribbean music is diverse and varies from island to island, but all of it has African and European influences. African influences include Syncopation of Cross Ribbon, Off Beat Accents, use of repercussion and signing styles. European styles include tenor, melodies, Bass, Key

Harmonies, and instruments such as guitar. Although Calypso music is often perceived as carefree and playful outside of the Caribbean, it has a deep political history. The genre originated from the struggle for emancipation and is characterised by its witty and imaginative treatment of themes such as racism, the Cold War, and the cost of living. Despite its lively rhythms, Calypso often contains subtle social interpretations.

Antiguan and Barbudans from the post-colonial era used Calypso music to demonstrate their objections against economic exploitation and class discrimination, to which they were frequently subjugated. Calypsonians typically associate themselves with a political party aligning with their beliefs and views. The primary focus of Calypsonian music was to promote messages of hope, freedom, and justice. The Calypso genre was the established form of music expressed in Antigua and Barbuda but was subject to the family background. For example, secular music was never aired in my household, and my sisters and I could never be heard reciting or dancing to Calypso music in the presence of our grandmother; she was an ardent Christian. We relied on a neighbour's transistor that played Calypso from the previous and current eras. Calypso music was in our genes, and those of us who could dance to the music did not hesitate to carry out expressions as was encouraged by the music.

Out of all of us, my fourth oldest sister had a good rhythm for the music and was a keen enthusiast. During a carnival season, she took it upon herself to sneak out and attend J'ouvert, hoping not to be discovered by our grandmother. Unfortunately, she got caught and was given a good cut-ass, and to this day, forty-five years later, she remains a fan of her cultural music and dance. My third eldest sister is suspected to be a good dancer, but she is a strict Christian and Conservative and would never be engaged in the crowd gathering by attending Carnival.

Regardless of the occasion, family and friends would have a beach day out, BBQs, fish, lobsters, stew meat, fried dumplings, litres of ginger beer, organic lemonade, and freshly juiced plum juice. Food and beverage were abundant with limited wastage, and being part of a family was not necessarily limited to kinship. Young people with their families would also meet at a beach during Easter.

My nearest and favourite beach is Jabbowack, to display our air inventions. The sky would be covered with a blanket of different coloured kites, which required skill by ground controllers to keep their kites in the sky without causing air traffic collisions and free from rapid descent to Planet Earth.

The time it took to walk to Jabbowack always seemed less than the actual time, as we entertained ourselves by singing Benna or telling stories; whatever the activity, there was always laughter and merriment; those were good, happy days. Laughter comes naturally for Antiguans, as it is soothing for the soul.

Antiguans are not governed by time but rather by the moment. Living in the moment allowed us to enjoy significantly life's moments more than being controlled by time. We believe that we are the owners of the time. Very few people own a watch or are dictated by it. Bad timekeeping or lateness does not appear in our psyche; the only way to be aware of being late is if events are finished, and participants have left.

If an Antiguan says, "See you in a minute", they invariably mean hours, and it does not necessarily mean that they are on their way. "see you in a minute" is a term of reference that I grew up hearing and knowing that it is not to be taken literally. As I got older, I struggled with this phenomenon, but conversely, I embrace difference, and equally, I would indicate to non-Antiguans to expect delays.

I used to watch Gaulins flying in the sky, which seemed very beautiful. They were free to roam the skies without restrictions. My life was like the Gaulins: whenever I saw one, it reminded me of my childhood days, when I had vast open space, bright blue skies, and scorching sun; my days were unplanned, unstructured, and not overly demanding.

Gaulins

Starting school-1965

Antigua and Barbuda offers free education to young people two to nineteen. It is optional whether parents expose their children to nursery school at two and a half years, but schooling is compulsory at five to sixteen years; Antigua and Barbuda mirrors the British educational system. Pupils start primary education at infant one and progress annually, though pupils who do not make the progression grade are held back for an extra year.

Pupils spend six years in primary education; after their primary education, pupils sit an assessment, influencing their progression to secondary school. My school building was a concrete frame shaped like an army barracks, the classroom had a high ceiling, and the walls were vacant and lacked pictorial decor. Antigua and Barbuda's literacy rates ranked at 98.9%.

I started primary school in September 1965; my day started at approximately 6 AM. I did not need an alarm clock, as the cock's crowing indicated the new day. My sisters and I had to go down to the village to get water to shower. Our shower involved filling a jack with water and a bowl used to pour the water from head to toe. I used to love pouring the water over my body because of the flowing sensations derived from the water and then washing the suds off whilst keeping my eyes firmly closed to avoid soap suds getting into my eye, but the shower experience was always invigorating.

The village school was situated on a hill five minutes' walk from NewWinthropes Village.

NewWinthropes School

Folks from the adjacent village, Barnes Hill, claim that the school is within their boundary, but NewWinthropenans highly contested that claim, and to this day, eighty-two years on, the school continues to be called NewWinthropes School. The school day started at 8 AM, and we did not dare to arrive late, as the headmaster would be waiting for us on the playground with a strap.

Therefore, the children from NewWinthropes would leg it across the field up to Judge's Hill. Of course, children's playful melee could be heard between the two villages. But, once reaching Judge's Hill and ringing the school bell at 8 AM, the chimes from the school bell could be heard between the two villages "Ding ah ling, ah ling, school bell ring".

All pupils would join the queue for their designated class group. There would be deafening silence; it was almost possible to hear the grass growing. A military type of inspection would take place involving checking fingernails. Boys' shirts couldn't be seen flying like a kite they had to be tucked in their Khaki trousers and polished shoes, face shine.

My memory of my first primary schoolteacher was that she struggled to deliver her subjects, and most of the time, she delivered her lessons through fear, a strap always seated on her shoulders which ascended on her victim's back from a height inflicting maximum pain or a ruler across learners' knuckles The teacher's insecurity, limited subject knowledge and classroom management were demonstrated by violence or verbal abuse towards her pupils. As a result, pupils were often referred to as dunces.

Numerous young people display various learning difficulties that often go unchallenged. Pupils with Dyslexia are often disadvantaged because the classroom teacher does not have the skill set to recognise it early or resources are limited to provide learners with the required support. A few years whilst I was on holiday in Antigua, there was a knock on the front door; a seven-year-old boy, a neighbour's son, came with his school books asking if I could help him with his school work., I was surprised by his requests as the young man was not known to me, nor was he aware of my profession.

I agreed to help the young man. I first looked at his English exercise book and the first line from his previous entries, I noticed that "February" was misspelt; the word was spelt with "d", and not a "b", which is a typical spelling error made by Dyslexia suffers, and as I looked further, there were other standard errors. I went to meet the young man's parents to share with his mum my findings; she confirmed that she was aware that he is Dyslexic and that the school was aware, but because of limited funds, he was not getting the required additional learning support.

So, with the young man's mother's consent, I continued tutoring him; I purchased some coloured paper to determine which coloured paper worked best for him. Once the method and resources were established, the young man enthusiastically and voluntarily appeared for the tutoring session every morning.

On another occasion, I donated some Key Stage books to a fourteen-year-old girl preparing for sitting exams. Later, I asked the young lady how she found working with the books, and she said, "I have learnt more from the books than the teacher."

In contrast, with my first primary school teacher, I had good exposure with a second primary school teacher who had a good rapport with us, whereby she did not impart fear and horror in her pupils who had entered the learning environment as novices.

Without a doubt, she was a well-rounded teacher who was both firm and fair. Her classroom was decorated with various posters and cards depicting different nursery rhymes, and she often displayed a blanket of images related to these rhymes. She always encouraged us to participate in storytelling and was patient with those still learning. Whenever necessary, she would retell stories repeatedly, and we listened attentively to correctly follow her instructions.

We repeatedly reviewed the nursery rhymes until we learnt them from memory; we could participate by reciting the verses or joining in with stanzas and actions. We loved this teaching method; we could exchange ideas and interpret meaning and pronunciations. These rhymes and stories invoke curiosity and questions, and wonderment. My favourites include Jack and Jill, the Three Little Pigs and "Hey Diddle, Diddle, the Cat and the Fiddle".

In that 'world', I imagined cats learnt to play the violin, cows could fly, and dishes could run. My favourite bible stories were Noah's Ark, Daniel in the Lion's Den and the birth of Jesus Christ. Our school celebrates the birth of Jesus, as He was the Saviour and King. The teaching of Christ taught us to be humble and helpful towards others.

Growing up in Antigua, I didn't hear many nursery tales, but I did hear a lot about Anansi. Anansi was a clever character who often got himself into tricky situations. In fact, his father turned him into a spider because of his cunning ways. I enjoyed Anansi's stories because they were entertaining and funny and taught essential lessons about self-reflection, discovery, and problem-solving.

When I first learned to write, I used a slate with sharp stone or chalk. This tool was used to develop handwriting, math, and spelling skills. However, the slate was unlike today's electronic tablets; we did not have any technology. Because of this, we had to rely on memorisation rather than being able to retain information on the device. We would wipe the slate clean to continue learning and move on to the next subject. The phrase "wiping the slate clean" comes from here, as it signifies a fresh start.

When we were young, we learned how to count using our fingers, with the help of our teacher's matchstick figures and catchy songs like "1,2,3,4, 5, Once I Caught a fish alive". After grasping the basics of counting from one to twenty etc. Our teacher introduced us to adding, starting with simple equations like one plus one. This same teaching method was used for subtraction and multiplication, and it was an effective way to learn how to count using our fingers and do mental math. We didn't have calculators or Google searches back then, so our only tools were our memory and fingers. However, we quickly became skilled in mathematics, but we knew memorising our timetables was essential.

I fondly remember Ms Spencer, my former teacher, who was likely in her early forties. She was a no-nonsense woman who would lead us in storytelling sessions where we would all sit in a circle. Ms Spencer would sit in the centre of the ring and play the role of 'Mama Hen' while we were her little chicks. She would narrate each story with great enthusiasm. Ms Spencer was a devout Christian who encouraged us to pray daily, learn scriptures, and sing gospel songs.

One of her favourite stories to teach us was the tale of Jonah and the Whale. One of my favourite songs was "Amazing Grace". We learnt each line of the song until we could sing it from memory. God's Amazing Grace surrounded us, our school was on a hill surrounded by natural beauty, and we could see the sea when it was rough or calm, hear an orchestra of birds chirping their songs and see the blue sky without a cloud and brilliant sunshine. Whenever I hear "Amazing Grace", I fondly reminisce on the day I was first exposed to the song.

Cooking Fuel & Utensils

Antigua and Barbuda display significant African cultural influence, predominantly from Ghanaian traditions. This influence can be seen in various aspects, such as music, language, arts and crafts. The national dish of Antigua and Barbuda is Fungi and Pepper Pot. In contrast, Chop Up, a breakfast dish made of pumpkin, eggplant, leafy green spinach, onion, and garlic, is also popular. The ingredients are chopped and sautéed together to create this delicious meal.

The dish is derived from the Arawak Indians and Africa and their cooking apparatus. In the event of a gas shortage or power cuts, a coal pot remains an essential cooking tool in Antigua and Barbuda households. Coal pots and Yabba predate Antigua and Barbuda's colonial era. They were occasions for golden opportunities to be formed as family members gathered around the cooking pots, heated by charcoal and waiting for the pepper pot, or stews, rice and peas, stew fish or meat to be cooked; the waiting moments created opportunities to reflect fondly and with pride on past generations. The elders gathered around the coal pots and took advantage of the opportunity to tell Anansi and Jumbie stories. The wait for the coal pots to complete their magic was worth it.

The Arawak Indians made far-reaching additions to Antigua's habitation in the areas of agriculture. For example, they were responsible for introducing guava to Antigua and Barbuda. Before Columbus sailed past Antigua, the Arawaks had established a system of government. They lived off the land, relied on herbal medicine for health purposes, and used herbs with cooking; they also had their mode of worship and recreational activities such as ball games. In addition, Arawak's words are still in use today, for example, maize, which means "bread of life" or "grain of the gods."

I grew up with food being cooked on coal pots. Coal was the only cooking method for most people in Antigua and Barbuda from the colonial era until the 1970s. The coal pot was also used to heat iron for clothes and iron comb. Charcoal is made from all types of wood stacked horizontally in layers of dried grass.

To make charcoal, the grass and wood are put in an earthen kiln in layers, and the process is repeated about three times. Next, kerosene is sprayed on the materials, and the kiln is covered with dirt. The kiln has two vents, and one of them is used to light it. Smoke will come out of the other vent once the kiln is lit. It can take up to seven days for the charcoal to be ready.

Charcoal kiln in the process of making charcoal

Charcoal

Coal pot, Bono Region, Ghana 2020

Coal pot, Bono Region, Ghana

Clay Yabba and Coal Pot, Antigua

Sugar Cane Planters and Reapers- 1965

My memories of school days go beyond the school's surroundings. I remember the cane fields spanned over fifteen acres, with countless sugar sugarcanes growing on either side of the road. These fields were part of Popeshead Head Estates in Judge, and many black men and women worked hard to prepare the soil and plant the sugar cane.

They used pickaxes, cutlasses, and hoes to dig trenches and endured the scorching sun. Despite the discomfort, they continued working with bags of sugar cane nodes wrapped around their waists. They would walk along the trenches, dropping a node in the ditch and covering it with soil to allow water to absorb in the channels. Women in long skirts, hats, or head ties would weed the cane with their hoes. By mid-December, the sugarcanes grew tall like giants, with feather-like bosky cane tops and lilac-coloured spears fluttering in the North wind breeze. The sugarcanes danced with melodious sounds.

On moonlit nights, storytellers would use dancing sugarcanes to tell Jumbie stories, leaving their audience fascinated by how something as sweet as sugar cane could be connected to Jumbie. Experienced elders had a sharp sense of when the sugarcanes were ready for harvesting, timing their harvest with the full bloom of June's flowers, also known as the Flamboyant tree. As children, we also knew that sugar cane harvesting was imminent when the majestic bright red flowers of the Flamboyant tree, locally known as June's flowers or shack, shack, appeared.

Harvesting Sugar cane

Flamboyant tree in bloom

Men and women would have sharpened their cutting tools, Bills, and Cutlasses while harvesting the sugar cane. A symphony could be heard from the rhythmical pattern of sounds from the Bills and those Cutlasses; men whistled, and women hummed. Sugar cane was a great delight for young people, young boys and girls willingly, industriously, and purposefully volunteered to help the older folks with stacking and tying the cane with cane leaves, after that stacks of cane would be taken to the side of the road and then packed onto sugar cane tractors and transported to Gunthorpe's Sugar Factory in Pigotts, which was about a mile and a half away from Popeshead Estates.

The sugarcanes were neatly stacked in piles and arranged flat on the truck floor, with an estimated size of nine by five. They were waiting to be dispatched to

Gunthrope, where they would be processed into sugar and rum suitable for the UK and other European markets. The child labourers who helped with the task were compensated with juicy sugar sugarcane. The children who participated were all from the same village and were between the ages of six and twelve.

Women Packing sugar cane to load on the cart

During June, we would eagerly anticipate the blooming of flowers. Additionally, we would keep an ear out for loud tractors that signalled their approach by their robust, sonorous sound. We would stay hidden until the tractor reached a certain point, and then we would remove sugarcanes from the tractor's centre, east, west, and rear.

Occasionally, drivers would try to speed up over the hump, but the weight of their load would often prevent them from doing so. As a result, we always aimed to remove the sugarcanes from the centre to create access for sugarcanes from the east, west, and rear.

Once the centre was loosened, it made it easier to access the sugarcanes, we would attack the tractor like birds of prey, and we would disappear with our prize position and disappear to our villages, Barnes Hill and NewWinthropes. Tractors would be loaded to the maximum. There were no weight restrictions; the tractors moved out from Popeshead Estate at a speed of fifteen miles per hour, which made it easy for us children to run down the tractors and pull sugarcane from its sides.

Most drivers didn't mind us taking some sugarcane for ourselves, but one driver would put his tractor in reverse to stop us. Despite this, we collected plenty of sugarcane from the other drivers, which made up for any losses. However, the cane juice caused our hands, clothes, and legs to become sticky, and we also got some minor cuts from the sharp edges of the cane. Despite these minor injuries, the reward was worth it.

In the early days of eating sugarcane, as a child, I was unaware of the evil association between sugarcane and slavery, its economic benefits for slave owners and colonialists who assumed great wealth from the free labour of slaves and cheap labours of 'freed slaves' who were 'paid' meagre salary for their labour Sugarcane was the main crop of the slaves. The salary earned was negligible compared to the wealth gained by those who exploited workers for their financial gain. Sugarcane workers worked under extreme conditions. Some sustained injuries and died in pursuance of their duties.

My molars were more effective at squeezing juice than the sugar mills. When my thirst for sugar was fulfilled, water was used to balance out the sugar; I remained energetic and lively throughout the day. However, when feasting on sugarcane delight, I was oblivious to my ancestors' plight and scars on the sugarcane plantation. For example, Harvard Law School was built off the backs of Antiguan slaves, and the sugarcane plantation owner Isaac Royall from 1672-1739, accumulated mass wealth from free labour.

As a child, I witnessed sugarcane workers toiling in the scorching sun without employment rights. Despite the sweat droplets on their skin looking like diamonds, it resulted from thirst and dehydration caused by their gruelling work. Sadly, many ended up crippled due to the perpetual bending-over required for sugarcane cutting. Although late, I've stopped consuming sugarcane or adding sugar to my beverages to protest its cruel history. It's a known fact that the transatlantic slave trade movements were created to develop and establish workforces for producing "White Gold" to meet the demand for sugar in America and Europe.

Slavery is not a bygone period, as the descendants of the slaves with the same DNA live on, and most of the descendants live in abject poverty. In addition, there are perpetrators under disguise who have made others become their victims of incest, non-consensual sexual encounters and rape. A practice that has blighted the Caribbean basin. These heinous practices from our bygone days, sadly, are current features. Yet, the majority of the time, brutes who commit these grotesque crimes often walk free and leave victims stigmatised and traumatised to face ridicule and shame that was imposed on them.

Chapter 3

Pre-Journey to London-1970

At age ten, I received the news of my departure from Antigua on 2/02/1970. Only a week before my departure, my grandmother delivered the information with a heavy heart and tears in her eyes. She told me I was going to England to join my parents, whom I had never met. The news was bewildering, and I was momentarily speechless. I protested and insisted that I did not want to go because England held no significance to me. I had never seen my parents, had no pictures of them, and had never spoken to them in my ten years.

While my sisters, nannies, and neighbours were thrilled, I didn't share their excitement when I found out I was being sent to England. I couldn't help but wonder if I had done something wrong to deserve this. The decision to send me away was made against my will, and I would have done anything to change it. Even though my grandmother tried reassuring me, I could see the pain and sadness on her face. It was hard for her to be separated from the "son" she had cared for, nurtured, and deeply loved since I was seven months old until I turned ten. Community members called me "boi fuh Mem." As the day of my departure approached, I felt increasingly anxious. Despite the reassurances of my sisters, Mama Juliette, my school teacher, and my neighbours, I was hesitant to leave behind everything familiar to me. Being brought up in a culture that values respect for elders, I found it difficult to express my concerns and objections. This made the experience very distressing and traumatic. I had no outlet to express my feelings and found it particularly hard as my maternal grandmother, who had always been my source of comfort, struggled to come to terms with our separation. Unfortunately, I had no access to resources - human or otherwise that could help me process these emotions.

The well-wishers endeavoured to appease me by saying that England was a magnificent country, that the pavements were paved with gold, and that they had a Queen that I might get to meet if I was 'good'. The tales of the well-wishers did not impress me as I was gratified with the dirt roads of my village, and the 'gold' pavements did not entice me either. England did not mean anything to me; young people of my age group never spoke about England.

Thus, I had yet to determine what I was going to do or what to expect. I was told that I was going to England. I had yet to learn of the climatic condition of the country. Because of the inseparable relationship between my grandmother, siblings and other profoundly loved ones adjusting to the idea of leaving them and saying goodbye did not abode well with me.

The union I had shared with them was about to be surrendered, not by my free will or through negotiations, but by brutal force. I was convinced they profoundly loved me, but I could not understand why they considered sending me away in my best interest. My grip was packed, and I showered in the open air for the last time. I sat on a rock and looked towards Jabbowack, the sea was tranquil, but my soul was like a troubled sea...I remained seated on the rock for at least sixty minutes with my indescribable thoughts, none of which I could recall to recollection.

There are unique homogeneous attributes of Empires, the Middle Passage era, Colonisation and Windrush. These factors have one thing in common, disunion; victims of the Middle Passage were forcibly removed from their hamlets, family and country of birth, and the purport of their removal was for free labour to create affluence in Europe and America.

Colonisation operated as homogeneous as the Middle Passage, though emancipated slaves were paid minimal salaries. Nonetheless, many families were separated during the era. The Caribbean Windrush propaganda derived from the publicising of misleading information spread throughout the Caribbean for workers seeking employment in the UK to rebuild the "Motherland." As a result of the promotion of the spreading of wrong information, many families were disunited in search of making a better life for their family and contributing to the "Motherland".

The psychological impact resulting from Windrush was similar to the experience of the Middle Passage assaults, where the treatment of victims fell below the level of humanity. The Middle Passage enslaved people were forcibly removed from their homes and forced into free labour, the Windrush generations were sold a false dream, and they left their homes and were exposed to exploitation.

In addition, colonialists demonstrated no interest in the consequentiality of black family life, denying children from bonding with their parents and forging long-lasting and stable relationships. The enslavement of Africans, Colonialisation and the Windrush have left a constant reminder of the plausibility of disunion.

Black families are often regarded as social entertainers, narcissistic, maladjusted, and malfunctioned. I had never been separated from my grandmother and sisters throughout my ten years in Antigua; I saw them daily. The idea of being separated from my loved ones was ill-considered, improper and ill-advised.

We shared our last family meal: macaroni pie and stew chicken. Although this dish is usually delicious, it didn't taste very pleasant this time. I cried throughout the meal and eventually felt better after finishing it. The meal felt like a way to face the impending loss of everything I had loved and cared for. It was hard to accept that I was about to lose it all without my consent.

After hugging me, my grandmother left our house and went to Mama Juliette's. Before she left, she instructed that I be picked up by the taxi from the east side of our property instead of the west. Mama Juliette's property is located at the bottom of our hill and is adjacent to ours. It was decided that it would be best for me to leave from the east to avoid the possibility of running into the two ladies who had been an essential part of my life for ten years and potentially missing my flight.

At 8:30 **PM**, a taxi arrived on the east side of the property. I walked down the hill with my sisters and Harty, giving a half-hearted goodbye to my neighbours as we made our way. As we descended, I couldn't help but glance at Jabbowack Beach, a place full of cherished memories. The airport was only fifteen minutes from home, but the journey was quite sad. I couldn't stop myself from being emotional the entire way there. This was my first time travelling outside of Antigua.

I arrived at Coolidge International Airport, now VC Bird International Airport, with my sisters and Harty, where we checked in at the BOAC VC10 counter. The checking-in clerk checked me in as an unaccompanied minor. After a brief wait, we heard an announcement from the speakers asking everyone travelling to London Heathrow to proceed to the departure gate. When we reached the entrance to immigration, my sisters and Harty handed me over to the airport staff.

BOAC VC 10

Despite my initial reluctance, I followed the airport staff. As I walked, I kept glancing back, hoping that one of my sisters or Harty would call me back, but unfortunately, they didn't. Eventually, I stopped and sat on the lobby floor at the Terminus, crying and refusing to go any further. I expressed my strong desire to return home, but after about ten minutes of protesting, I reluctantly agreed to continue. As I slowly walked with the airport staff towards the giant bird sitting on the tarmac, no one was walking in front or behind me.

Once on the tarmac, I glanced back to the airport terminal and my sisters, and Harty were standing on the balcony waving; I waved back. For a moment, I was overtaken by an odd feeling, which was virtually surreal, but the entire event was surreal. But what might have appeared as a dream was a reality. Finally, I had reached the point of no return, I glanced back, tears running down my cheeks, and I gave the final wave to my loved ones.

I was escorted to my seat by an air hostess, and the situation in the aeroplane was eerie and frightening. The windows were small, and there were many white people on board. I saw more white people in five minutes than in a year or longer. I couldn't recall seeing any other black people, but it's possible others were there but not in my section. I felt uneasy after being led to my seat on the aeroplane. It was a new experience, and I was still determining what would come next. The feelings of happiness and freedom were replaced with confinement and loneliness as I sat alone with strangers around me.

A loud, unfamiliar, unexpected roaring noise was heard when the door of the giant bird closed. I was still crying and feeling agitated and unsettled, especially when the stewardess came to strap me in. I protested because I didn't want to be restrained or shackled, but I noticed everyone else was strapped in. In my village, we often speak of patients being put in a straitjacket, so the experience was even more unsettling. I was told it was for safety reasons.

I heard a loud noise that sounded like a roar, and the giant bird started crawling slowly. I had no idea what was happening. The noise got louder, and suddenly, the bird took off and flew up into the sky, leaving Planet Earth behind. As we continued our journey, the noise gradually decreased, and eventually, Antigua disappeared from view. I felt like I was embarking on a purposeless trip into the unknown and overwhelmed with a sense of helplessness. I couldn't help but cry.

Chapter 4

London 10th February 1970

I travelled from Antigua, a small Leeward Island in the Caribbean, to meet my parents in London. Unfortunately, I had no information about the weather and was unprepared for how cold it would be during winter. Thankfully, my Harty gave me a jumper, which came in handy, as I had no idea how I would have survived the harsh and bitter cold without it.

Antigua is known for its beautiful beaches, fantastic weather, and friendly people. The temperature in Antigua during February 1970 was between twenty-four to twenty-eight degrees, starkly contrasting London's chilly and windy two-degree weather. This was a significant adjustment, as I was used to a much warmer climate.

On February 10th, 1970, I finally arrived at London Heathrow airport, approximately one thirty in the afternoon, London's time, after an eight-hour journey from Antigua's Coolidge Airport. As I stepped off the plane, I was taken aback by my new surroundings. My new home had been chosen for me by well-meaning adults, but it wasn't my choice. The first thing I saw was a grey sky and shiny ground that didn't exactly live up to the phrase "the streets are paved with gold". The colour of the sky and earth were almost matching, both platinum in tone.

A flight attendant brought me to a line where I had to wait to see the airport doctor to certify that I could enter the UK. While waiting to be examined, I blew smoke from my mouth without a cigarette, which was a strange experience. It was freezing, and I couldn't feel my fingers and toes. The line was next to an outer door, and a fiercely cold wind greeted me every time it opened. It was a coldness that I had never felt before. I was shaking, and my teeth were chattering, but I couldn't warm up no matter how much I shook. Unfortunately, my clothing wasn't suitable for the climate of my new home.

Before meeting the doctor, I constructed a story: I was taken from my home against my will; I was suffering from a headache, and I could not take the cold; England was not my home. Despite my hopes that a strong argument would allow me to return to Antigua, the doctor declared me fit, insisting I would eventually acclimate to life in England. But how could I adjust to a culture and weather so different from my own? I couldn't deny my love for Antigua and its culture, which remained the most crucial aspect of my identity. I refused to forget my ten years of living in Antigua and couldn't imagine ever denying my Antiguan roots.

I was utterly distressed by the ordeal, which commenced when I was told that I was going to England, disunion from my home and my loved ones and being handed over to strangers, travelling to England as an unaccompanied minor. It was a perplexing experience. I convinced myself that I had done something wrong and that the traumas I had encountered resulted from my wrongdoings, which I could not account for. No one appeared perturbed by my tears. It might be because they, too, were struggling to come to terms with their traumas.

After the visitation to the doctor, I boarded a BOAC coach destined for London, Victoria. It was my first time on a coach as large as the BOAC coach and the driver speaking over a microphone, a significant contrast from getting on a twelve-seater bus in Antigua. The coach left Heathrow Airport, heading to Victoria; The coach passed vast open spaces and fields covered with sleet blankets.

I was in awe of what I saw because I lacked knowledge of sleet. I'm used to seeing morning/evening dew with a sparkle of silver, which is typically wet, but I've never seen it frozen before but never set in a solidified state. Coincidentally, the sky was dark and bleak, and the face of the sun was nowhere to be seen. I gazed into the sky, looking for the appearance of the sun, but instead, I saw mass upon mass of grey clouds. I needed to understand where I was and why it was so arctic compared to the weather in Antigua.

Of course, I was mesmerised by the Victorian buildings that I thought were factories with small towers on top, which were gushing out plumes of smoke. Initially, I thought the buildings were on fire without flames, which intrigued me even more, and there was no sign of fire officers attending to the structures on fire; I wondered what type of hell this was. Houses in Antigua were painted with vibrant colours. The houses were spacious, with ample yard space. I later learned that the little towers were chimneys used as outlets for fumes from burning wood and coal.

London Victoria-1970

The BOAC coach arrived at Victoria Station at approximately 5 PM. By that time of the day, it was dark, the sky was lightless, and the weather was freezing. I disembarked and was directed to customs and Immigration. I was granted clearance to enter the United Kingdom. I arrived in the country where the pavements were supposed to be paved with gold, but my own immediate experience proved otherwise. It was the starting point of apprehensiveness and dubiousness.

Upon entering this unfamiliar land, I felt like an alien. The sky was grey, and the wind blew fiercely, whistling like a speeding vehicle. I lost track of time and paused briefly after clearing Customs and Immigration. I questioned what I had done wrong to end up in this hellish place. All I had were my parents' names, no photos, phone numbers, or addresses.

Displacement symbolises slavery and has remained a part of our inheritance. It is not difficult to relate to the feelings of the slaves from the Middle Passage period who were taken from their homes, the land of their birth, and children wrenched from their mother's arms, causing ongoing displacement and, ultimately, slaves being sold to the highest bidder.

Selling of slaves

Chapter 5

I was approached by a man who asked if I was Jovan. I responded in the affirmative, and he introduced himself as my father. My father, I thought, I don't know you, I have never seen you in ten years of life, but suddenly you are my father. I have never referred to any man as my father, but here I was, confronted with a new situation. I have a father.

My father had in his hand a duffle coat which he gave me to put on, it was a very welcoming gift, and it offered some warmth from the biting cold elements. I inquired about my mother and was told, "She is home." For a brief moment, my soul came alive when he used the word "home," which I equate with Antigua, and I enquired if she was in Antigua. He responded in a matter fact manner, "No, this is our home" ... our home, I thought to myself, it is your home, not mine. My parents lived in Pimlico, a ten-minute walk from the BOAC terminal.

The walk to their abode was freezing, long and comfortless. I struggled with the notion of the pluralised word used, "our". I wondered at what point I was made part of the amalgamation referred to as "ours", especially as I was never asked or consulted. Nonetheless, I had to learn quickly to live with the integrated trauma of living with strangers. I masked and suppressed my feelings of hurt and anger and embraced a new home.

My biological mother did not raise me; therefore, I, naturally, had no recollection of her. Conversely, my maternal grandmother was my 'surrogate' mum. I was ecstatic with my mum; I had no preconceived idea of my parents or what England was like. I was inundated with fear and anxiety with the meeting, as anyone would with strangers. On the other hand, my grandmother on my mother's side acted as my substitute mother. I was overjoyed to be with her and had no prior notions about my actual parents or what living in England would be like. However, meeting my parents for the first time filled me with fear and anxiety as they were strangers.

My father and I reached the street where they lived in a two-bedroom Victorian house in Pimlico, London. All the houses on the road had a similar design - they were terraced, painted in a dull grey colour, and appeared to be joined together without any space in between.

The street was quiet though people were moving about, they passed each other without awareness or exchange of salutation, and my father and I encountered several scornful stares, which I guessed was a standard appearance for white people.

My father opened the front door, separated by the pavement from the road. I was intrigued when he opened the door without knowing what to expect next. The inside of the building appeared more sizeably larger than it looked on the outside. The building was divided into three levels: a single person occupied the ground floor, a family was on the first floor, and my parents occupied the second and attic floors.

We entered the living room, which was open plan and incorporated the kitchen. As I entered the living room, I saw a large lady in the kitchen. As it is customary in Antiguan culture, I said good evening and the large lady responded and enquired about my grandmother and my sisters, and I assured her they were ok. Once those pleasantries were over, she turned her back and continued with what she was doing in the kitchen.

I stood in anticipation to be greeted by my 'mother' with, at the very least, a hug. Still, I was confronted by a slab of frozen ice and an icy reception identically to the temperature on the outside. My father saw the uneasiness and called my brother, my brother. I did not know I had a brother before that moment, nor did he. My father told my brother to take me to the bedroom I shared with him. My brother and I were baffled, as we had no idea of each other existence before the cold icy reception.

My brother asked where I had been for the past seven years of his life. Furthermore, he had yet to learn that he had four sisters and a grandmother in Antigua. The entire experience was freaky. I was shocked and taken aback by the reception I got and the revelation of a brother I did not know of. Within less than twenty-four hours of my journey into the unknown, I encountered at least seven traumatic shocks that left me wondering, "What have I done?" I took away from the cold reception that I was not welcome. I wanted to turn around and head back to Antigua, and if it were possible, I would have...coming to London was not for me. Cold on the outside and cold within the abode.

My brother was born in the UK and is the youngest of my parents' children; I am three years older than him. Despite my brother's apparent confusion from the impact of the bomb that our parents had dropped on us, he endeavoured to make me feel welcome, more so than my mother. He was enthused to know about me, Antigua, our grandmother and our sisters. I struggled with embracing the warmth and friendliness shown by my brother.

I was mindful of the restraints of being in an odd country and the revelation of a brother of that I had no prior knowledge of. The challenges that appeared before me were enormous. In Antigua, I was the youngest among my siblings, but in the new family sector, I was the eldest within the family hierarchy, and at the same time, I had to live in a unique situation. The entire situation seemed daunting and puzzling, as I did not know my brother like I knew my siblings I grew up with in Antigua.

Additionally, the environment was different from what I was used to. The houses were all the same in design. People appeared to be squashed up together; the freedom of young people was restricted to a mass of concreted areas, with no open spaces where young people could go and socialise with each other. Whereas the young people from my village all belong to the same kingship. There were many open spaces where we could socialise, and there was a natural flow between us.

I was mentally exhausted from the changes from beginning my journey to arriving in England. I was still trying to understand the coldness that I sensed from my mother and how neither my brother nor I knew each other. The environment was equivalent to hell, the weather was freezing, and the exchange between my mother was icy and, at worst, an appalling nightmare. She showed no traits of my grandmother, neither in her personality, stature or mannerism.

Mother Input

My mother had partial sight. She had cataracts, which caused her vision to be fuzzy. She refused to have her cataracts operated on, and I did not know how long she had been diagnosed with the condition. She tended to tilt her head and read with one eye closed, but I believe, at times, she missed essential information. She often relied on others to read and write for her. Writers would have the task of re-reading her dictations. She was an attentive listener, asking the writer to rephrase in areas that needed to be amended.

I was the fifth child of my mother, as she had four children before meeting my father. She and I never warmed to each other. At all times, I perceived her to be very stern. Therefore, I did my utmost to avoid getting her upset. At times, I struggled with knowing what would be acceptable or unacceptable. On occasions where I have erred, it would result in her, at best, shouting at me and, worse, in physical punishment with her hand, broomstick or any other instruments that would cause severe pain as was intended.

It was ostensible that how she would punish my brother and me was different. She mainly threatened him, but it was a constant brute force with me. Evidently, her demonstration of love and appreciation was not equally demonstrated. I struggled to come to terms with her demeanour towards me. Equally, I worked with my feelings that leaned towards intense disliking for her because of my Christian upbringing to "honour your parents", but the bizarre situation I found myself in where I did not feel valued or loved was a severe challenge to my Christian beliefs.

After supper, I was told by my mother to wash the dishes, and she introduced me to Vim and Brillo pads to scrub the pots. The pot bottoms had to be shone. Otherwise, it was a case of continuing scrubbing and applying more elbow grease until the bases were sparkling. I scrubbed the pot bottoms, partly tired and sleepy from my long journey. However, sleep was a long way off. After the ordeal with the pots, my brother and I were told to dress up because we were going out. The idea of going out with my mother and brother was exciting to the point that I thought my assessment of her was wrong.

Evening out-1970

My mother, brother and I arrived at the bus stop for an unknown journey, our father did not join us on the mysterious outings, and I did not dare to ask where we were going, plus I was too tired to care. The evening was much icier than the afternoon upon my arrival at Heathrow Airport. There were few people at the bus stop. I was surprised that no one greeted each other, as would be the norm in Antigua.

However, I was bemused by the peculiar dancing some people performed. There was no music being played, and in those days, iPods or mobile phones were not invented, but the dancers were hopping, shaking their shoulders and hands. I looked in astonishment and wondered what that type of dancing was called. It was so cold. I was tempted to bop to the phantom rhythm. I need help understanding how people could be out and about in arctic weather. The intensity of the weather was far more than I could tolerate, and it was another dilemma that I could not adjust to.

After what appeared to be a long time of waiting, a substantial red double-decker bus, number 24, arrived. My mother, brother and I boarded the bus. At first, I thought we were boarding a spaceship, and I was preoccupied with the bus's layout. It had seating upstairs predominantly for smokers and downstairs for non-smokers. The bus differed from the single deck twelve seater cramped buses in Antigua. Sitting upstairs provided a more panoramic view of London. As passengers settled in their seats, a conductor moved up and down the gangway, saying, "Fares, please."

The presence of a bus conductor was unknown to me, as we conventionally pay the driver at the end of our journey. My brother and I shared a seat, and our mother sat before us. I noticed the bus had made several stops on its route and would stop when passengers pressed the bell or stuck their hands out, signalling the driver to stop. Bright lights were to be seen everywhere, but they offered a divergence from the dull grey sky.

It was all a mystery, travelling on a double-decker bus with bright lights and traffic flowing in two lanes. My personal tour guide, my brother, pointed out places of interest, most of which meant nothing to me, but nonetheless, my knowledge grew, and I gained insights into areas of importance in London. Victoria was home to many red buses that serviced London, tube and train stations and coach stations.

Many red buses were iconic and travelled to different parts of London. A number of the buses showed at the front and the back their ultimate destination. The buses were the cheapest form of transport used to transport its citizens to their place of work. Therefore, visitors to London benefitted from the bus ride. Albeit I was tired to the point of exhaustion, I was in awe of the sights and the commentaries received from my brother, who had a good knowledge of London.

I was tempted to put my head above the parapet by asking if a bus would go to Antigua. It might be better to keep quiet, as our mother could hear our conversation. However, I could not see that possibility given the geographic and climate differences. London appeared to be an extraterrestrial, intriguing and busy city with many places of interest. But, on the other hand, London makes NewWinthropes appear to be sleepy. At 7 PM in NewWinthropes, most people would be off the streets, and the only light that might be visible would be light from hurricane lamps. At 7 PM UK time would be 3 PM in Antigua.

Hurricane Lamp

Chapter 6

Final Destination-1970

Finally, we arrived at our destination, John Lewis- West End. John Lewis is a departmental store with many floors, and it is situated on Oxford Street, Oxford Street is known for shopping for people from all walks of life. We arrived at John Lewis at about 6:30 **PM**, but the street was packed with people hustling to get somewhere. We crossed over the road to Hanover Square, entered a building and took the elevator to the second floor. I was fascinated by the function of the elevator, as I had never seen or been in one before. I had encountered many facets of life in less than twenty-four hours that were diametrically different from my life in Antigua, and I was sure there were many more surprises in store.

My mother used a key to enter the office suite, and my mother handed me a black bin bag and a damp cloth. I commenced a vocation as a cleaner at the age of ten and less than eight hours of being in the UK. My brother and I had to cover the entire office floor, empty the bins and ashtrays, and wipe them out with a damp cloth. What a contrast to my laid-back life in Antigua. She vacuumed the carpet area.

The vacuum was another new gadget, as I had never seen one before, as floors in Antigua were swept with a broom. I learnt to use a mop and mop bucket for the first time. I left Antigua with no expectations, but the exposure to life in London was an education in more ways than one without being in a traditional learning environment. I followed orders methodically, mindful that I had no choice but to do what I was told, as my mother's silence was eerie. She very infrequently smiled or laughed.

Myth

Having a choice has never been the prerogative of black people. Our selection of determining our skin colour was defined for us, our designations were imposed on us, and the types of jobs we pursued were imposed on us. Accessing education was imposed on us. The Windrush generation was duped into believing that the "Motherland" was the route to achieving a "better life." The verbalisation, "London streets are paved with gold." The verbal expression derived from the story of Dick Whittington and his cat. Whittington and his feline friend arrived in London expecting to discern the streets covered in gold, but instead, the streets were filthy, unhygienic and depressingly deprived.

Many Windrush generations were optimistic about the untold possibilities in the "Motherland." It's possible that the Windrush generation would have been more equipped to handle life in the UK if they had been presented with a more accurate depiction instead of the overly optimistic idea that the streets were "paved with gold."

It was very noticeable that the people employed doing office cleaning were blacks. It was assumed from the observation that the work the blacks were hired to do provoked my thinking by wondering if that was what was meant by rebuilding the 'Motherland'. The building my mother worked in had several floors; most employees were predominantly black women, but the supervisors or managers were white males, mostly white females.

The absence of native whites engaging in cleaning suggests that they scorned the idea of doing work that they perceived as degrading. As offices had to be cleaned, individuals from the Windrush generation who came to England from the Caribbean to rebuild the 'Motherland' and make life better for themselves had no choice but to accept the work that natives did not want to do.

Recruiting blacks to come and work in the 'Motherland' was reminiscent of colonialism, where black people toiled the sugar plantations in readiness for harvesting the 'White Gold' and it was the blacks who worked long hours in the scorching sun for a paltry sum of money to make ends meet. Black Caribbeans responded to false propaganda that engendered a picture of prosperity in the minds of those individuals who bought an erroneous dream.

Yo-Yoing

Throughout the first seven hours and after that from being in England, my parents never asked how I felt whilst I was yo- yoing between being fearful about entering an unknown world and its many unknowns; I felt very solitary, perplexed, isolated and dispirited. My life took a forty-five-degree turn. I missed my grandmother, my sisters and my home environment.

We arrived home at approximately 9:15 PM. It appeared that my father was already in bed. I went to have a shower. The shower set-up was vastly different from my open-air shower. It was designed for the environment and suitable for its inhabitants. Nonetheless, I had showered and was heading to the bedroom. Still, before I could reach the bedroom, my mother called out to me, redirected my footsteps to the bathroom, told me to wash my briefs and socks every evening, and promptly said, "You are not in Antigua now."

I took her warning to mean I had to do my laundry, whereas, in Antigua, my sisters did my laundry. Finally, I got into bed at approximately 9:45 PM from the ordeal of events that had engulfed my thoughts from the moment I arrived in the UK. My brother had slept off. I got a weird sense of confusion whilst sobbing. Where actual events overtook me turned out to be a terrible nightmare; everything seemed strange, my parents, relying on paraffin heaters to keep warm, hanging wet clothes on a line above the bath. It was a peculiar habit, as I was used to seeing clothes on a line in the yard.

Great efforts were made to comprehend the hell I was in and what I did wrong to end there. When will I arouse from this dream, or will I ever?

The office cleaning followed a Monday-to-Friday rota, or Saturdays were exchanged for Fridays for several months. I got no thank you for my efforts, but I kept doing what was expected.

At ten years old, I had chores that I carried out after school. I had to cook for the family. Saturday mornings, I would travel on bus 36 from Pimlico to Harrow Road to buy ground provisions, as my father only ate yam, green banana and dasheen. Unfortunately, these food items could only be purchased at a stall on Westbourne Park Road, off Harrow Road.

I would have returned home with the shopping, unpacked the things, and placed them in their designated area. A pile of clothes was waiting to be ironed...there was no rest for the wicked. I had very little spare time, was kept busy perpetually, and had to clean the living areas, toilet, and bathroom. I took strength from Paul Robson's song: Ol Man River, Show Boat 1936, like the indentured black workers; I too got "weary" but kept on going. Bedtimes were always a welcoming change from my laborious chores.

Negativity 1970

I arrived in the UK with a limited reading ability and the skills to read fluently. Moreover, I spoke with a deep Antiguan Creole accent. My mother and I visited a cousin with children of similar age. Our cousin's children were born in the UK. After the introduction, my mother said abruptly, "He can't read". Apart from being shocked by my mother's remarks, her audience appeared thrown not by my weaknesses but by the mortification that she had caused me to suffer in the presence of people I was meeting for the first time.

While my mother and cousin were in the kitchen, the children and I had a great time in the living room. My mother's absence did not bother me much, and the children were friendly. They showed me a variety of storybooks, and the brother and sister alternated reading to me. The stories were captivating and even encouraged me to read myself. Although I was hesitant, they patiently helped me sound out difficult words and used "jump beats" to break down the words into manageable parts.

The time with my cousin's children was well spent, as I learnt a reading technique. I was encouraged and wanted to make progress with my new reading skills.

The time spent with my grandmother and sisters prepared me to hold my own in any situation and not be overtaken by other people's lack of encouragement. The problem that occurred at my cousin's home was not of my making, it was imposed, but the way I was nurtured and my culture were sufficient to avoid focusing on the pessimism of others' deeds and fixating on the positive.

I recognised and was aware of my limited reading abilities; I, however, wanted to work on my areas for improvement. My mother's introductory comments showed me up. The embarrassing situation created new meaningful possibilities that opened doors for me to learn a new reading technique that helped develop my reading ability.

Chapter 7

School 1970

I commenced primary school on 17th February in Victoria. It was a very miserable cold morning; I was a ten-year-old. I was born and raised in a suburban village in sunny Antigua. The landscape of my village was picturesque. One was surrounded by natural splendour, a magnificent sea view depicting an endless flow of deep radiant blue. The plant life was always luscious and green, with birds singing on their tree tops.

Oh, how I missed my home. In contrast to my village, the scenery of Pimlico consisted of endless rows of terrace houses stacked together with miniature towers on the top of the houses bellowing out grey smoke; that I had never experienced before, it all appeared very eccentric; it was positively different. The entire environment appeared grim, the trees were bare, and the people were robotic, going to and fro without interacting with their fellow human beings.

Momentarily, I mentally considered absconding, but I quickly dismissed that thought as I reflected on the cut ass, I got previously for endeavouring to run away. The school building, the classroom, the pupils and the teachers were very different from what I was used to in Antigua. So, I was surprised when I was introduced to a woman dressed in a long black gown, a black head scarf, a white collar and a long chain with a cross around her neck. She turned out to be the school's headmistress. My first reaction to the sight was, "Lawd, ah wah kine ah el mi deh inna?" I have never met a white head teacher before and not to mention a Catholic Nun. I have never come in contact with anyone from the Catholic religion in my entire life. So, there was a cryptic feeling about the school facilities, a nun as a headmistress, dressed in all black, except for the white collar and a long chain with a cross, it all seemed very gothic and different.

Following the introduction to the headmistress, I walked through a long corridor with high ceilings. The ceilings and the walls were painted a dull grey colour, which was coordinated with the colour of the sky. I walked past several rooms painted in deep blue with numbers written in white. The classrooms each had their door, not with room dividers as in Antigua. Extraordinarily, the desk and chalkboard resemble the ones used in Antigua. I was momentarily excited to see something that reminded me of home.

The classroom teacher, not dressed in all black, introduced me to the class. My appearance aroused curiosity along with many questions. No pupils have heard of Antigua, peculiarly, that included the black pupils. It appeared that the only place in the Caribbean known to most English people was Jamaica, whilst others had yet to learn of the Caribbean hemisphere. One boy inquired if we ate people in Antigua, and before I could answer him, the teacher digressed and asked me to take my seat. The question offended me, and I genuinely wanted to tell him about his r**** hole. The classroom was comprised of male, female and black and white pupils, which was another oddity to me, as I have never been in a school where black and white pupils were taught together.

The learning programme was similar to Antigua, but worshipping took the form of reciting the "Hail Mary" ... I wondered what they were discussing. Some had a cross in their hands. It was all foreign to me. I struggled with participating in their mode of worship, as I was accustomed to praying to Jesus and hoped He would deliver me out of the hell that I was in.

After the worshipping, the teaching and learning commenced, followed by milk and recess, teaching and learning, dinner break and recess, teaching and learning, and the end of the school day. The lessons being taught appeared less challenging than what I was accustomed to in Antigua, and in Antigua, we never got a free bottle of milk.

Despite that, the teacher made me feel like a dunce because of her difficulty understanding my Antiguan Creole language and my limited reading skills. On the other hand, I had no problem understanding her, but she always left me feeling like a square peg in a round hole.

The first few weeks of being in an English primary school took some time. Some things were unfamiliar, like having a bottle of milk every morning. I would gently peel off the silver cover and gradually slurp away at the cream, which I loved because of its sugary taste. I was not overkeen on the main body of the milk because it tasted watery. The school was enclosed with part wall and high metal fencing with a heftily black ponderous iron gate which was always locked whilst the school was in progress, which was an unfamiliar sight, as in Antigua, my primary school had no fencing, but the buildings were locked at the cessation of each day.

We would go to Renee, a vendor, during recess in Antigua. Her facility was a two-minute walk from the schoolyard, and she supplied us with the obligatory sugar rush that would see us through the school day. Her sugar cakes were sweet and well-flavoured with different spices and essence. She had all sorts of confectionery delight, but mine was her sugar cake. Fascinatingly, at the catholic school in Victoria, there was no street vendor outside the school campus, and we were never allowed to leave the school premises until home time.

I looked outside and witnessed a massive down pouring from the sky of white fluffy elements. I was astonished by the immaculate white fluffy elements and carefully watched them fall to the ground and become a solid mass. I told the boy beside me, "Look, cotton is falling from the sky". He rebuked me, saying, "Don't be silly; it's snow". The class erupted with laughter. The teacher restored order and mitigated my mortification for not knowing what snow was. She told the class that there are countries that do not have snow.

At playtime, pupils appreciated the presence of snow, and many of them engaged with rolling balls with their bare hands, the white fluffy element, which I later learned was snow. Many of the pupils lobbing the balls at each other appeared unaware of the freezing temperature, and there was lots of laughter and exhilaration. Unfortunately, I was not ready to participate in the activity. Nevertheless, it was nice seeing snow for the first time. Cars were covered, snow enveloped the bare trees, and roads were thick with snow blocks.

Albeit the snow appeared nice, I was freezing just from being on the playground, and my fingers were numb without physically contacting the white fluffy elements. I did not require convincing that I would not participate in what appeared to be playful, though I was clothed for the cold climatic condition. I found myself shivering like the Winter dancers. Some pupils endeavoured to entice me to join their pastime of lobbing snowballs. Some made a snowman and attempted to convince me that it was not freezing. I declined the invitation and thought that if it were not freezing, I would not want to experience it. I asked myself, "What would be freezing to them?"

England was a cold place; much more arctic than any coldness I have ever felt. On the outside, water freezes and turns into ice. People engaged in doing the Winter dance. Most people were clothed in warm Winter clothing such as sweaters, jumpers, gloves, coats of various designs and sizes and multiple types of foot ware, boots and shoes made for the climate with cold winds, sleets and snow.

There were air vents that blew hot air from inside to outside. I placed myself next to one of the vent outlets to keep warm. I was not alone, as few other black pupils did the same. I never participated in playground games, and it was too arctic to be chasing after a football, and the white pupils excluded the black pupils from taking part. There were occasions when some of the white pupils would pass by and spit on the ground where I was standing and say, "Golliwog go back home".

Most of the time, I did not understand what they were saying, but their faces showed contempt, so I inferred that they were being aggressive towards me, but I could not understand for what purpose. I had inquired from my brother about the meaning behind the word "Golliwog". My brother showed me a picture on a marmalade bottle depicting an image that represents a "Golliwog".

The picture depicts a black face, broad white lips, white eyeballs and frizzy hair, like someone who had come in contact with a ghost. I struggled to understand why anyone would refer to black people as a "Golliwog". I learned that individuals with those mind set are white people who don't like black people. But, conversely, I did not understand why they said "go back home" when England was supposed to be our "Motherland".

Initially, I did not understand the meaning behind the name-calling. Still, when I became aware, I was perplexed and resentful at the thought that my humanity was acknowledged by my skin colour and not as a person. During the Middle Passage era, an Anglican Bishop confirmed with an inquiry when asked if it was ok to kill slaves. His response was, "Yes, because they have no soul".

The Bishop's response indicates that racism was a part of the English DNA, where black people are marginalised and discriminated against because of their skin colour and not as people with similar human feelings. We eat food when we are hungry; we feel pain when hurt; we grieve from suffering a loss of a loved one. Coincidentally, I was not required to be told or reminded that England was not my home. Albeit I was far away from Antigua, Antigua was still my home. The explanation that my brother gave, I was filled with utter contempt for the English, I did not understand them, and I did not care to understand them either.

I struggled with coming to terms with accepting the name callings to be a part of the host's way of life, and by living in England, racial indifferences were a component of their fabric, which I wanted no part of it. I kept myself from being around English people socially, although I recognised them as human, just like me. In Antigua, racism was not a component of our fabric. In the village, its population was black people. In my primary school, we were all black people, so detesting another race was not an option. We were taught to love one another, an inherited legacy from our predecessors from the colonial period.

I abhorred being in the school, detested being in London, and found nothing that genuinely impressed me. I was perpetually aware that my skin colour was a threat. I struggled to find comfort in living in a harsh, cold land.

England was much more arctic than any coldness I have ever encountered.

Chapter 8

Change Gonna Come

There were many occasions that my mind travelled to my school days in Antigua, recounting the times when my peers and I would dash out of the classroom, heading for the vendor for our sugar rush; my favourite rush was brown sugar cake we snacked out under a tree where we sat telling jokes, socially teasing each other, we enjoyed each other's company, and upon hearing the ringing of the school bell, we would race each other back to our class.

Those moments enabled me to deal with the hostility and name-calling. I avoided letting anyone see my teardrops and letting on that I was missing home, a place where I was regarded as a human and not a colour. As a result, I shed many teardrops but found my inner strength to stand up to the bullies. I was no longer prepared to allow myself to be a victim of racism. Instead, I decided to fight back and match verbal abuse with verbal abuse and physical violence with physical violence.

The day came when the playground bully passed by next to the vent where I was standing; he spat on the ground and said, "Wog go back home"; I responded by spitting on the ground and calling him "white honky". He appeared shocked by my reply and approached me with aggression. I received my first box in my face from a white boy with a tightly clenched fist; I landed him a thump in his mouth, blood was pouring from his mouth, and the playground came to a standstill. Cold notwithstanding, I stripped down to my vest because I was determined to put licks in his skin.

I was escorted to the head teacher's office, where I was made to feel that I was the protagonist and not the victim. I endeavoured to explain myself, but my explanation fell on deaf ears. I endured weeks of name-calling from that boy, but strangely no one heard him or witnessed him spitting at me, but everyone noticed and saw my reaction. I was given a stern warning from the lady in black, but from that day, the bully and his entourage avoided me like the plague.

I am perpetually grateful for my upbringing, grandmother, and Northern people who endured tribulations during the colonial era. Despite the difficult times and harsh treatments, my people consistently demonstrated the vigour of Hercules Pillar (Galleon Bay, Antigua), who were resilient and tenacious. I did not leave my village to become a victim of racism or to allow myself to be bullied. On the contrary, I learned not to take on the weaknesses of others, especially those who had a problem with my blackness, because it was not my blackness they really were afraid of, but rather, the DNA of my slave predecessors, my spiritual and cultural heritage from which my moral compass was composed, my unbreakable spirit of striving to achieve better for myself and keeping my self-dignity despite the odds.

London, London, the streets were covered with black snow, with a biting cold breeze and no evidence of the roads being paved with gold. Whoever made up that story was a daydreamer. I hurriedly walked to the house; my toes were solid as rocks, even with two pairs of socks. I could barely feel my fingers; I wondered what the hell this was. I finally got to the house, and it was nice to be inside in the warmth. My mother was in the kitchen, her back facing the living room, sitting on a chair.

I greeted her, and I could see steam coming from the pot; I assumed she was cooking...she did not respond to my greeting but said, "Jovan, come here," with her back still outwards to the living room, her voice tone was flat it was difficult to discern anger. I walked up to where she was seated, wondering what wrong I had committed. She turned around and grabbed me by the collar with a firm grip; she grabbed hold of my right hand with her left hand still holding my neck and asked, "Where is the money you stole?". At that point, my fingers were inches away from being immersed in the pot of boiling water.

Instantly, my entire body went into a seizure; I don't know if I had bladder or bowel movement first, but I do know I experienced both whilst at the same time stating, "I did not steal your money," it was a harrowing experience, the hold around my neck was released. Still, it was exchanged for blows to my side, head, and face whilst my fingers were dangling inches away from touching the water.

I was extremely fearful of her immersing my fingers in the pot of boiling water. I eventually owned up to a crime that I did not commit with the hope she would release my fingers, she finally released her hold, but I endured beatings for several days, and she demanded to know what I did with her child benefit money. I had no idea what Child Benefit was. I was in the UK for approximately three weeks, and before coming to the UK, I had never heard of that term or its benefits. I took the blame while the guilty culprit walked free.

The person who went to the post office, forged her signature, and cashed the money remains a mystery. It was puzzling because the household consisted of my father, an alcoholic; my brother, who was seven years old; her, the victim of the crime and I, a novice to the UK. The culprit remains unknown today, but I believe she knew I was not the thief in her heart. Instead, I got the blame because I was the lowest-hanging fruit. I perceive similarities of being the lowest hanging fruit with the Africans who were brutally taken from their homeland to the "new world" as they were the lowest hanging fruits as their Kingdoms were already operating in slave trading, which made it easier for the Europeans who studied the natural environment to exploit the situation.

Harty, one of my nannies, gave me a souvenir dairy with the flag of Antigua printed on the front cover with a pen. I cherished the gift because it was given to me by Harty with love, as well as it had Antigua's Coat of Arms on the cover, which was a constant reminder that I was an Antiguan, not that I needed reminding. My parents found the diary in the bedroom that I shared with my brother; it was not hidden, but the content was personal to me. I used to enter things that I found valuable and consequential; one of my entries was my trip to Westminster Public Library and my first reading book.

My parents called me to the sitting room, my mother was sitting around the dining table, and my father was next to her. My first consideration was that I had done something wrong that I didn't know about... I timidly approached them and said 'yes' as I recollected the slap I got previously for saying "yeah." Their faces suggested that something was about to go down, and my heart was beating fast. My father presented the indictable evidence of my diary and demanded to know where I got it from; I told them Harty gave it to me, and after that, my mother asked me to explain the entries, which they had obliterated beyond recognition. I told them that from recollection, I wrote about my visit to Westminster Library and my fascination with the many books available to readers.

My mother, the Judge, asked why did I make those entries I did not have an answer. My father took the pen from the diary pocket and broke it into two with a firm warning to make no further entries. The impact on descendants from the Middle Passage era has affected family lives; it removed individuals' rights to be independent, oppressed individuals and divested them of having the right to privacy. Slaves were expected to comply and adhere to the enslavers' rules. Similarly, young people who were descendants of the bygone slave days were nurtured and expected to comply with their parent's rules. Most of the time, imposed decisions often leave victims traumatised with stark despair.

The diary was returned to me. I left my parents' presence feeling violated, as they had minimised me to nothing. I thought I had no rights, no freedom to explore my individuality, and I was left without my independence, as their authoritarian parenting obstructed my growth; deep down, I believed a change would come one day.

My bother introduced me to Westminster Public Library, ten minutes from the abode. I became a library member; the library appeared like an Aladdin cave with numerous books. I was fascinated by the countless books of all descriptions and for all ages. The first book I have ever read in my ten years was "This is the House Where Jack Lives" by Joan Heilbroner. The story was perpetual but engaging; it outlined the house's occupants with clear pictorial images supporting the text. I found the book user-friendly because it was easy to read and a stepping stone for exploring other books.

Chapter 9

Scapegoat-1974

G rowing up, I noticed my mother's apparent favouritism towards my brother, whom she called her "handbag". She showered him affectionately, using his nickname "Lio," they would frequently embrace, kiss, and laugh together. Although I longed for a similar relationship with her, I learned to keep my emotions to myself since she didn't appreciate my unique qualities or personality. One day, I asked for a hug before my mother left for work, but she turned me down, saying, "Not you," before walking away. After that moment, I stopped trying to win her affection because she treated her children differently and had no interest in developing a close relationship with me.

1974 I was fourteen years old, and my fourth eldest sister came to join us in the UK. She was five years older than me and eight years older than our brother. I was excited by the reunion with my sister, whom I had bonded with from birth until I was ten. My sister and I got on very well. My mother did not hesitate to let my sister and me know that we were outsiders within the family.

An example of this was demonstrated one Friday evening. There were two tubs of mousse in the fridge; my sister told my brother he and I should share one, and she would have the other; my mother said matter-of-factly, "No, he does not share you, and your brother should share." My sister and I were stunned by what was told to us. My sister did not bother taking the mousse, and I declined.

My mother and sister argued a few weeks after the incident. My mother did not take kindly to my sister arguing back with her and picked up one of my sister's shoes and hit her over the head, which resulted in my sister receiving three stitches. My sister is not the type that anyone would assault physically without retaliating, she responded, and my mother sustained similar head injuries. After that, the relationship between the two of them remained cold.

Despite the coldness between my mother and sister, my sister had a better relationship than I had with my mother. My sister and brother would outwardly disagree with her without any consequence; on the other hand, I had learnt the art of avoiding confrontations with her. Moreover, I was vigilant of the distinction between my siblings' relationship with her and mine; they had bonded with her from birth, and my mother did not raise me.

My parents had a toxic marriage, and they were evidently unhappy. I have no recollection of them demonstrating their love for each other. She endured his drunken and violent outbursts. Verbal and physical outbursts were an ongoing occurrence between them. I was never clear about the factors that triggered them. My mother was not a drinker or a smoker. My mother was responsible for maintaining the abode; she often had to single handily make decisions on important issues, such as keeping a roof over our heads.

It was evident that the functioning of the household would have collapsed if not for her. My mother's behaviour towards me may be due to her trauma from living with a violent alcoholic husband and feeling ashamed of his addiction. Apart from my father's alcoholism, I envisaged her struggling with relocating from Antigua to the UK for a better life as well as dealing with issues with childbirth without having access to the supportive network that would have been available to her in Antigua. Apart from her endeavours to find a better life, she may have struggled with adapting to the climatic differences from the one she was accustomed to in Antigua.

In addition, the difficulties experienced in the host country where black people were marginalised, experienced racism, cultural differences, finding employment and being disempowered by the system. It is not my intention to excuse my mother's behaviour towards me but to attempt to understand the trauma and difficulties she was confronted with, which may have influenced her decision-making and led to irrational judgements. Unfortunately, my relationship with her was filled with hostility and unexplainable blame.

She accused me of things I didn't do and spread false narratives about me being "bad" despite never explaining what that meant. The treatment I received was intolerable, so I ultimately ran away. When I was ten and my brother was seven, we broke into the gas meter and stole two shillings. My brother came up with the idea, and I broke the seal. Our mother punished us, but for some reason, she always mentioned my name when talking about the theft.

I struggled in the British education system, which I attribute to my parents' failure to prepare me for the differences between it and the Antiguan system. It was a source of shame for me not to know how things worked in British schools. I felt ashamed to have ended up in the care of Westminster Social Services accommodations, but what my mother failed to mention was that her deliberate actions were the cause.

She made me feel unwelcome and like an outsider, causing me to change my name from Jovan W O'Brien to William Henry. At 14, my mother stopped buying me clothes and gave me five pounds when I needed new shoes. Despite searching every shoe shop on Oxford Street, I couldn't find any shoes for that price. However, Freeman Hardy Wills had a basket of discontinued shoes, and I had to settle for a pair of burgundy platform shoes that were a size too small, causing bunions. My sister from Antigua sent me two parcels to help, but my mother took what she wanted for my brother, violating my trust.

Following the period I spent in the care of Westminster Social Services accommodations, I spent many years not speaking with my mother. I blamed her entirely for what led to my admission into the care system. My mother spent years decrying me as a terrible person. I visited her on one occasion while she was sick, a friend of hers was with her when I saw her, and she introduced me as the "prodigal son". I was offended by the use of the term "prodigal son".

When I was forced out of the family home, I did not go out because of something I had done and returned later because I was sorrowful for my wrongdoings. I did not leave the family house with belongings that were not mine. I went with the grip that I left Antigua in 1970. I left because of her wrongdoings toward me. She has never accepted or acknowledged her faults. She was very skilful with creating drama between her children. My late grandmother left a wooden house for my eldest niece and me.

I had sentimental attachments to that house because I grew up there. My eldest sister sold the house to a friend in 1977 without consulting me; when I heard about the house sale, I requested its return, as it was not my sister's house to sell. The friend, my sister, sold the house to claim she had done some repairs and consequently asked for more money than she had paid for the house.

My sister did not have the money to pay to have the house returned. She contacted my mother, who sent her the money and instructed her to collect receipts in my mother's name; once the house was returned and the receipts were in my mother's name, she told my sister, "Tell Jovan he no longer has a house."

I was annoyed with my sister for selling my house in the first place, and she did not recognise her wrongdoings; she excused her actions by saying that the house needed repairs. In addition, my eldest sister (maternal) takes the view that I must have contributed to the harsh treatment that I encountered from my parents by being "baderation and mischievous".

I sustained head injuries for asking a neighbour to stop exchanging her dead landing bulbs for ours. Additionally, our mother dragged me from my bedroom by my testicles, bit out my knuckles down to the white tissues, beaten me in the head with a heavy crystal glass astray for reminding her that it was my brother's turn to do the laundry, run, which left me dripping blood like a sheep at slaughter. However, my eldest sister is not known for making sound judgements. One of her bad judgments involved selling the house that I was raised in. Her terrible decision caused our mother to deviously repurchased the house and removed me as the owner because my grandmother had not left a written will.

My sister's remarks suggested that the assaults that I got from my parents were because I was either "mischievous" or "baderation". My father slapped me across the face for answering "yeah". Our mother had my fingers dangling over a pot of boiling water, and she cut me in my head with a table tennis bat, causing an injury of three inches. The assaults occurred from age 11-14.05

My eldest sister resides on the property of our late grandmother and is where most of our mother's children were born. A six-foot post-Arawak stone structure was on the property that held history for each of us; my eldest sister had the structure demolished without a trace or consultation with the rest of her siblings.

My mother's input did not come as a great surprise, as it was in keeping with her resentful and nasty attitude towards me. Many years have passed, and I have never received an apology from my mother. In 1976, I left boarding school with a clear agenda that I would never live with my mother. I had moved away from my mother, and at that point, my parents had already separated – it may have been a legal separation. My father had a flat in Ladbroke Grove, while my mother lived in Lisson Grove, Baker Street. Luckily, Vaney allowed me to stay with her until I found a job, and for that, I was grateful. However, Vaney's bitterness and mischief caused problems. She told my mother I planned to set dogs on her- a false accusation. My mother, unfortunately, did not care to hear my side of the story and charged at me like a raging storm. She grabbed my chest and twisted my shirt collar, but I managed to push her away. As I tried to leave the room, she blocked the door. She charged at me again, and I firmly pushed her away with all my strength. I reminded her I was no longer twelve but sixteen and would fight back. Finally, I left Vaney's house and started heading to my sister's place. My mother followed me to my sister's home, ten minutes away.

My mother lacked compassion and has never been interested in my happiness and well-being. I had two experiences of being forsaken by my mother; the first time occurred when I was left with my grandmother, and the second time of being placed in the care of Westminster

Social Services; on both occasions, I received no emotional support from my mother, I grew up not knowing the heartfelt appreciation of a mother. Although I did not reside with my mother, I used to visit to clean her windows and vacuum her abode, where she and my brother lived.

Despite the odds, I continued endeavouring to get acquainted with my mother to the point that I allowed myself to be manipulated by her. I received a phone call from my mother in 1989, which was highly odd; my heartbeat and mind chased away with apprehensive prospects wondering what the purpose of the call was. She wanted to borrow three hundred pounds to assist my eldest sister in travelling to New York.

Coincidentally, I had just commenced a saving account and did not have the money to loan to my mother, she begged and pleaded, and reluctantly I caved in and took three hundred pounds off of my saving account with the clear understanding that she would repay the money the following week. However, the next week came, and my mother declared that she did not have the money to pay me; subsequently, my saving account was closed, and she died fifteen years ago without paying that debt.

I was aggrieved that my mother refused to repay the money; the final learning curve for me was that I realised that, irrespective of my effort, my mother would never accept or treat me as her son. I would never have a son-to-mother relationship, so I built a wall to protect myself by having nothing further to do with her.

My son was born in 1986, and my mother has never put herself out to visit or to get acquainted with my son. So he grew up without knowing his paternal parents. In 1995, my son attended Sylvia Young Drama School on Saturdays, opposite my mother's house. Usually, I used to offer private tuition on Saturdays in East London, but one particular weekend, I had to give additional tuition to prepare students for their SATs test. This meant I would be late for my son's drama class. I asked my mother if she could take care of him until I arrived in the evening, and she agreed.

This was an excellent opportunity for them to get to know each other. However, a few days later, my fourth eldest sister informed me that our mother accused me of using her to look after my son. Naturally, I felt upset and disappointed upon hearing this news. Since then, I have not taken my son to my mother's house, and he has not shown any interest in visiting after his first encounter.

Despite the hardships and setbacks, I managed to pull myself up from the depths of despair. I completed a two-year course, which I obtained a certificate from the Central Council and Education in Social Work; I hold a Level 3 Diploma in Flour Confectionery from the University of the South Bank, an MA in Adult Education obtained from

Goldsmith College, Level 3 Diploma in the English Language. Additionally, I have published an article in the Education Journal: Forum Vol.2, Number 1, Spring 2000, about using Creole Alongside Standard English to stimulate students' learning. With twenty-eight years of teaching experience, I spent eighteen of those years at a top London college, which has received two awards for excellence in education from the late Queen. During the time of the awards, I was employed at the college.

When I was twenty-one, I visited my mother, who was lying in bed. I apologised to her for any wrongs I had committed against her and also wanted to clear the air about not being the thief who stole her Child Benefit money. I was previously too scared to bring up the topic, but I felt it was necessary to be honest with her. So I told her, "I did not steal your Child Benefit money." She responded, "You didn't?" I affirmatively responded with a firm "No".

She pulled the duvet over her head and turned her back on me. I left her room without knowing what to make of her protective cover of hiding under the duvet. I later learned about the intended purpose of Child Benefit, which was paid to parents bringing up a child or children. Ironically, my mother had received this benefit for five years on my behalf, yet I had never received any of the money.

At least monthly, my mother would pack a parcel I would take to Vauxhall Bridge Road Post Office to send to my eldest sister and her two children in Antigua. My mother paid for my sister's children's education. I had often carried parcels on my head, as they were too heavy to carry by hand. Taking the boxes to the Post Office was embarrassing, as I was the only person walking the streets with goods on my head, but I had to get them to the post office.

Family separation can impact family lives and their decision-making process. My late mother died and was buried in London. She was put to rest on 23rd January 2009; the day of her funeral coincided with the marriage of her eldest grandson, who got wedded in Antigua. My eldest sister did not attend the funeral and stayed in Antigua for her son's wedding.

Language Conflict 1971

Growing up, Antiguan Creole was spoken in my community and culture. However, when I started attending British schools, my strong Creole accent was viewed as a "Mumble Jumble" language by my British teachers. This made my first few weeks at St Thomas Moore Secondary School a nightmare as my classmates and form teacher found it difficult to understand me.

Despite having an American teacher from New York, Ms Susan Jaine, I still struggled to communicate with her due to her difficulty understanding my cultural language. I tried my best to speak the "Queen's English" but had no idea what that entailed. The conflict between us continued for weeks with no end in sight. It's important to note that Caribbean Creole originated from European slave masters denying slaves the right to speak their language, demonstrating their power over them.

Slave masters did not value the cultural existence of enslaved people. They allowed one tree to grow naturally while uprooting and replanting another in different soil, causing it to take longer to mature. The enslaved people's use of Creole was unique because they combined the European language with their "mother's tongue," showing that two languages could be used and raising morale.

I struggled with giving up my language and culture when my form teacher insisted I speak the "Queen's English" and referred to my language as "Mumble Jumble." I did not want to lose my identity and self-worth, but I also wanted to learn. I avoided conflict with the form teacher by taking unauthorised leave from her lessons.

For centuries white supremacy has subdued the development of black people, controlling their natural spirited nature of being autonomous and keeping blacks subjected to the 'superior' system. On the occasions when black people protested against their oppressors, they were imprisoned, placed under house arrest and labelled. My enrolment at St Thomas Moore lasted for a maximum of two months; Ms Jaine and an educational psychologist diagnosed me as being "maladjusted" and recommended that I be referred to a school where the classes are smaller than mainstream educational facilities.

I spent five years in school in Antigua. I was not defined as "maladjusted", and there were no issues with being in a learning environment of twenty pupils or more per class. However, my culture and race presented challenging concerns for those with power. The authority with the power overlooked that I was new to the country and the emotional traumas that I was going through with being removed from my homeland and brought to another country where everything was vastly different to what I was accustomed to, meeting parents who were absent from my life for ten years, meeting my brother for the first time. I was disadvantaged by not having no pre-introduction to schooling in the UK, nor any support with the accepted form of communication in line with the "Queen's" English.

When I moved to the UK from Antigua, nobody asked me how I was adjusting to my new life. It was assumed that I would naturally adapt, but I needed help to leave everything I knew behind. I felt traumatised from being separated from my family, friends, and way of living. I struggled to adjust to the cold and grey weather in London. Neither my parents nor I understood the term "maladjusted" .... and its negative connotations. We accepted the school's classification and recommendations without question. Unfortunately, the school never gave us a copy of their expert report, and we didn't realise it was our right to receive one. My form tutor and others at St. Thomas Moore should have discussed my cultural background or offered support.

Chapter 10

Deeds of Wickedness-1974

My brother and I had weekly tasks that we rotated; for example, one week, one of us would take the clothes to the launderette, and the other would clean the apartment. "Thunderbirds Are Go" was my favourite cartoon, which used to come on Saturday mornings. The Friday night, I stayed up and cleaned as it was my brother's turn to take the clothes to the launderette. My mother allowed my brother to go out to play and left the laundry behind. I took my shower, and while moisturising my skin, my mother stood by the bedroom door and said, "When you finish, take the clothes to the launderette".

I thought she had forgotten that it was my brother's turn. I calmly and respectfully reminded her that it was my brother's turn. She instantly charged into the bedroom like an out-of-control bull, grabbed me by my testicles and dragged me into the sitting room; she dropped down onto the sofa still with a firm grip around my testicles, the pain was excruciating, and she released her hold of my testicles but locked me in between her legs.

My father had a thick glass ashtray on the coffee table, and my mother picked up the astray and beat me in my head and back. The astray dropped, and she gained hold of my left hand and bit out the outer protective skin of my knuckles on both hands; she bit the skin down to the white tissue that protects the knuckle bones. Fortunately, my sister was at home and came to rescue me; when my sister saved me, I was dripping blood like a lamb being slaughtered. My sister accompanied me to Westminster Children's Hospital for treatment. Unfortunately, my sister minimised the truthfulness by telling the doctor and nurses that I was in a fight.

I was discharged from the hospital with solutions to treat my injuries to protect against infections. My sister and I had no idea where we were journeying from the hospital. We were apprehensive about facing our mother, as we both feared additional attacks from her. In addition, London was a new environment for us; we were unaware of any services we could contact for help, nor were there any extended family members we could call upon.

I left the hospital feeling drained, mentally exhausted and confused from the events, which caused me to end up in a hospital emergency room. There were more questions than answers. I was grateful that my sister was at home to save me, as I feared I would have been killed; as the beatings to my head were severe, I was going in and out of consciousness. I was utterly helpless.

My sister and I were lost in a foreign world and living with a mother whose temperament was explosive. I continued to suffer from head and back pains. The only available alternative for us was to camp on the stairs of the apartment building. My sister and I camped on the stairs for several hours into the night.

Finally, my father arrived maybe after 11 PM and inquired what we were doing on the stairs, my sister explained what happened, and I showed him my hands and the swelling to my head. He appeared visibly distressed and told us to come and let us go inside; my father went first, followed by my sister. I followed her but was highly cautious about entering the apartment for fear of further unexpected violent outbursts, as I had no idea what frame of mind my mother was in.

Nonetheless, we entered, and my father asked if we were hungry; we answered "yes," and he asked my sister to go and prepare something for us to eat. My father went to his room without finding out from my mother what caused the injuries I sustained from her hands. It was assumed that my mother was in the sitting room as she did not appear, and my brother was not in the bedroom I shared with him.

So my sister and I ate in her bedroom. I had limited use of my hands from the sustained injuries.

My sister washed the dishes, and we went to bed. I stayed awake for most of the night crying and reflecting on my contributions that caused me almost to lose my life. At first, she may have misunderstood my intentions in reminding her that it was not my turn to take the clothes to the launderette. But, genuinely, I could not come up with any other explanation to justify her actions.

The incident replayed continuously in my mind like a stuck record player needle; I was stuck for answers and found it difficult to go forward. My fourth sister told me some years later that my mother was angry with me because she believed I was informing folks back home of the maltreatment I was enduring. I never once discussed with anyone of the problematic situation that I had gone through.

Heritage

Before meeting my mother in Antigua, my father had three children in St Lucia, two boys and a girl; the girl was his eldest child. Therefore, I was his fourth child. As he was an alcoholic, he would go on a drinking binge from Friday afternoon until late Sunday afternoon. He frequently appeared to be emotionally uncertain, more so when drunk. Sometimes he could be good-humoured, but it could never be assumed to be the general rule.

He was originally from St Lucia; he was six feet two inches; his mother was a Caribbean Indian; I have never met or seen a picture of her. I met three of my father's brother who resides in the UK, one out of the three endeavoured to get acquainted with me, he asked questions like what life was like for me in Antigua, and he was a good listener, but the other two were neither here nor there. My father's siblings were spongers. They relied on him primarily for their bread and butter, one of his brothers lived with us, much to my mother's displeasure. The one that lived with us was very much a lady's man; he had one lady that was regarded as the "wife", but in between, he had many more ladies on the go.

My father was a typical man of his generation in the Caribbean, where there were distinct gender roles. He never questioned this cultural norm and assumed his role as head of the household and breadwinner. He was a disciplined man who adhered to strict schedules, leaving early in the morning and returning late in the evening. Occasionally, he would administer punishment based on my mother's requests for misbehaviour on my part. He also had some handy skills, like decorating, and my brother and I would assist him in stripping wallpaper and mixing paste. However, my mother was solely responsible for household chores like cooking, cleaning, and laundry. My father was deeply rooted in his traditional ways, inherited from his ancestors.

Living with him was a rollercoaster ride of emotions. Sometimes he was in a good mood and would affectionately call me "Gigi," but his happiness was fleeting and could quickly turn sour. I always had to be cautious and watch for warning signs. I suspect he called me by that pet name to maintain control over me and prevent me from feeling secure in our relationship.

Living with him was incredibly unsettling, and it felt like I was constantly walking on eggshells. I avoided disagreeing with him, as even positive comments could be taken the wrong way and cause him to become easily offended. Despite struggling with alcohol addiction, he secured a job at the GLC works department. I never asked about his job; I knew better than prying. He would leave for work every Monday morning like clockwork.

It seemed my father could only focus on 1 thing at a time. Unfortunately, he has never accompanied my brother or me to parent-teacher meetings or medical appointments. He is known to have had several siblings and was the eldest among them. He occasionally talked about his sister Silica or my namesake, Jovan, who he also spoke fondly of. There were no pictures of his siblings, but there were some photos of my brothers from St. Lucia.

Unfortunately, I have never seen a picture of my paternal grandparents, as none were displayed in our home.

My father always dressed impeccably, with well-groomed hair and prominent dimples. He wore suits for every occasion, with well-fitted trousers and a trilby hat. He had a trilby for work and socialising and was a man of few words. My father fitted the stereotype of a "saga boy" perfectly. He was a womaniser who didn't hesitate to sleep with his wife's best friend. However, he sometimes astonishingly referred to his wife as Mrs O'Brien.

He declared this maybe to demonstrate 'ownership' or let other women know he was already married and the patriarch, the alpha male of his home. His womanising lifestyle symbolised the slave era, where slave masters would have their wives who resided in the 'top house.' Still, the slave owner assumed the right to have any female slave provide him with extra sexual exotic conquests. Sexual exploitation was not new, as the raping of black women occurred on the Zong, on plantations and during the Windrush era.

Degrading women were not restricted to my father's brother, as my father operated similarly. My mother had a Jamaican friend that she referred to as her 'daughter'; on Friday evenings, the lady would visit when she knew my mother was out at work under the disguise of bringing shopping for my mother, but in reality, the lady came so that she and my father could get intimate. She would engage in small talk with my brother and I. She would say goodbye to us; my father disguised himself as the 'perfect gentleman'; he would see her to the door.

My brother and I would wait awhile, sneak out of the living room, quietly lean over the bannister, and watch my father and his "Godmother" engage in questionable behaviour. My brother was offended by their actions, but I found it amusing at first. However, as time passed, I became traumatised and disgusted by what I witnessed.

It was challenging to process whether it was real, and I was too scared to tell my mother. My father acted like nothing had happened when he returned thirty to thirty-five minutes later while my brother and I watched TV. I found their behaviour disturbing and had never seen anything so dishonest like it before, as it was not commonly seen in Antigua, where I grew up with my grandmother and sisters. My maternal grandfather died when my mother was one-year-old so, I was not raised in a household with a male figure.

My father consumed lots of alcohol to the point he walked, moving back and forth. Additionally, he was a heavy train smoker; he self-rolled his cigarettes, and his preferred brand was Old Holborn. Apart from his weekly playing of the Littlewoods Pools and maybe on the horses, he was not a compulsive gambler. He always took advantage of a Lucian Jamboree. On special occasions, when going to an all-night party, he would iron his shirt and trousers to his standard while dancing to the beat of Jim Reeves. My mother was never invited to those events; he would be gone until Sunday evening. We would only get invited to his family functions, birthday gatherings, or weddings.

He was known to be spitefully hostile; he and my mother frequently got into physical fights. My first exposure to domestic violence was horrific, as I had never encountered events where a man would beat a woman. On one of their fighting outburst, I wanted to intervene. I was ten, but my brother advised against it because fighting was their regular feature. On another occasion, he endeavoured to stab his wife in her throat, but she blocked it with her arm, and she subsequently had to run out into the street to avoid him.

I knew my father's drinking habit was not conducive to his health and mental well-being, and I knew how he staggered around was not good either. My father's drinking habit was a new phenomenon, as I was not raised with alcohol; it was very different. What was more astonishing was watching him staggering and being incoherent. I felt utterly helpless, upset, and worried from witnessing the adverse impact that alcohol was having on him; not only was I concerned for him, but I also lived in ongoing fear for my safety because of his explosive temper.

Unknown to him and my mother, I had endless sleepless nights; I was tirelessly distressed because of my home environment. On the occasions when he was inebriated, lit cigarettes would drop on the floor, and the sofa caused me to be fearful that he might unwittingly cause the house to set on fire; I was apprehensive about him cooking on the stove because infrequently he would leave the gas on and fell off to sleep.

The list of concerns was endless. I walked to school feeling drowsy and, at times, too mentally tied to absorb what was being taught. My father's siblings were aware of his alcohol addiction, but none offered him support on quitting, but some were heavy drinkers too.

Chapter 11

Searching for Home February 1970

When I arrived in Victoria, only my father came to meet me, which I found odd given that we had not seen each other in ten years. Instead of comforting me after my long and exhausting trip from Antigua to London, my mother focused on teaching me how to clean using Brillo and Vim and commencing office cleaning. They seemed unaware of my emotional state and showed no concern for my well-being. I managed to stay awake despite my mental exhaustion, but my parents didn't ask how I felt during the first seven hours of my arrival.

By the second week, I realised that my reservations about their unfriendliness were justified when my father slapped me across the face for responding to him with "yeah" instead of "yes." His hand stroking my face echoed like water against the side of a rowing boat. I was left dazed, speechless by the unexpected slap that left the printout of his fingers across my face. The assault I endured symbolises the rigorous treatment our slave ancestors tolerated from their plantation owners, which is passed on to generations.

My father had the opportunity to bond with me by teaching me about UK's acceptable manners; instead, the 'slave man's personality took over. As I examined the welts across my face, I was filled with resentment, exasperation, and hostility towards him and, ultimately them. My grandmother, who raised me for ten years, has never beat me, and this man, whom I have only known for approximately two weeks, had already left his physical marks.

Following the day, my father gave me a slap across the face. After that, I held no desire to be in London, and my desire to be here became less attractive. The abuse left me feeling violated and aggrieved for a very long time. I planned for several days to run away and find my way back home to Antigua. In May 1970, it was approximately 5 PM; it was still visibly light.

I decided to find Antigua and sneaked out of the house in shorts and a T-shirt without shoes. Although I needed to learn the local area better, I was determined to reach my destination. I asked several people for directions on how to get to Antigua, but they had no idea where Antigua was. Some even mistook it for Montego Bay.

My frustration grew as my attempts to find my way continued. My search for finding Antigua took me only as far as Victoria. Eventually, I decided to head back to Pimlico on foot. As the evening grew colder and darker, I realised my clothing was inappropriate for the temperature drop. Some people I asked for directions noticed my shivering and suggested I go to the local Police Station on Horseferry Road, but I declined. Ultimately, I had to abandon my quest to find Antigua and returned to Sussex Street, Pimlico, at around 11 PM.

I got to the house but was afraid and reluctant to ring the bell. Instead, I went down to the basement and lodged between the bins. Unknown to me, my parents and the Police were looking for me. My father spotted me between the dust bins and called "Gigi." I was taken in by the softness of his voice tone and the reference to my 'pet name.' I answered and went up to the street level. A Police Panda car coincidentally pulled up, and my father indicated to the Police that I was found safe and well. The Police drove off without speaking with me.

My father assured them I was safe and well, but little did they know I was anything but safe and well. My father escorted me upstairs, and when we got into the living room, he ordered that I remove my shorts and my y fronts and bend over a dining table chair. Next, my father whipped me with an electric wire flex; each lash sent the pain of fire throughout my body to the point I had no control over my bladder that I P***** on the floor; each lash made a sound equal to a pack of card placed against a rotating fan blade.

I cannot recall the number of lashes administered, but I can remember the excoriating pain I had endured for months and the remaining scars. The experience was traumatic; I was left with rage and hurt. My mother did nothing to stop the beatings. For years following the assault, I wondered if that was the norm for punishment in London. The experience left me with psychological and physical scars for many years. As the years rolled by and upon reflection on that awful day, I equate the beatings to what enslaved people had experienced.

The slave masters utilised a whip or other weapons to keep the slaves in their place of bondage. Off-springs of slaves carry the DNA of their slave predecessors. The ancestors learned their discipline style from their slave masters, which has become a generational legacy that subsists in black communities today. While some might argue that slavery is over, regrettably, that is not the reality for many blacks whose parents maintain the outdated and colonial methods of disciplining their children that are seen and regarded as 'discipline enslavement', where black children's voices are not heard.

1970s Police Panda car

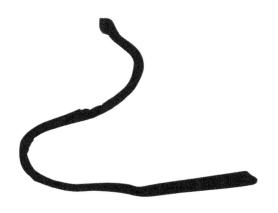

Slaves' whip

Chapter 12

Boarding School-1971

What education did I receive from my boarding school?

I started boarding school in November 1970 after being excluded from St Thomas Moore RC School, Chelsea. Louis White, who was supposed to be the English teacher, was more interested in teaching us criminal activities than anything educational. He often used a set of keys to show us how to pick locks and break into cars. Despite being given a writing book, he never taught us grammar or sentence construction.

Unfortunately, many classmates would sneak out of school at night to commit burglaries in the local community. Shockingly, Mr White would often buy the stolen items from the pupils. As a result, I didn't learn anything useful in Mr White's class and was disappointed with the lack of education provided.

Some teachers were aware of White's misbehaviour but chose not to address it.

The following year, I was in Fred Ransom's class. He was a dedicated teacher who worked hard to bring out the best in his students. But unfortunately, he struggled to work within the school's strict rules regarding teaching "maladjusted" learners. Ransom only lasted one term, but before he left, he told me that I had potential and could attend a grammar school with my parents' consent. My mother, however, refused to spend money on it.

Furthermore, the shower facilities at the school were communal and always left open without privacy. The staff even supervised shower time, with one teacher standing at the entrance for a prime view. This made me uncomfortable and vulnerable. The experience was uncanny, they were not only 'supervising' the shower period, but rather it was a period for fulfilling their fetish fantasy of watching a group of adolescent boys showering and, more concretely, fulfilling their exotic dream of watching naked black boys.

It was noticed that they did not just take an unfocussed glance, but their stare was more fixed like an eagle's on its prey; their eyes were fine-tuned on the boys' genitals area. They treated the period as spectators' sport. Infrequently, they gossip about boys' penis sizes and ridicule their victims' mortification. The covert sexual invaders were labelled as 'pervs.'

I would often take a strip wash to avoid entertaining the sexual invaders' fantasy, which invariably resulted in me walking to the headmaster's office for being 'challenging'. I came across to the headmaster as exasperating, and my resistance to being exposed to odd people did not abode well with me. Amazingly, the headmaster agreed that shower curtains could be used, ending the spectators' sport.

It was common for me to visit the headmaster's office. When I found situations objectionable, I would firmly let my voice be heard and often to the exasperation of the house parents or teaching staff. The exposure gained from being self-educated allowed me to demonstrate my proficiency in using the Queen's English; I was so proud of myself that I could relate to those individuals in the same native tongue as those who once ridiculed and described my Creole language as 'Mumble-Jumble'. Once the staff knew my ability to code-switch from Creole to Queen's English, I shifted from being a 'Mumble Jumble' speaker to a barrack-room lawyer and having a chip on my shoulder.

At fourteen, I was fascinated with the writings of Eldridge Cleaver, Soul on Ice. Cleaver was a black civil rights campaigner; he campaigned against the wanton killings of black people and made it clear that black lives matter. A houseparent found the book in my bedside locker and took the book to the headmaster. I was summoned to his office, and he asked why I read a book about a 'rapist'.

I told the headmaster that I was uninterested towards his convictions or the label attached to him by a white legal system, but rather to stimulate my mind and awareness of the struggles black people face daily. The headmaster banned me from bringing the book into the school and advised that I should stop reading the book. Of course, I returned the book to the village library, but I continued reading it there.

I did not stop reading the book, which would not be in keeping with my personality; obviously, they were something about the writer that spooked the headmaster. I suspect the headmaster was disturbed that Cleaver could demonstrate that the confinement could not break his spirit.

Protest

Back in 1973/1974, the country had a food shortage. The headmaster decided to ration the sugar and bread intake, but he and his family were still eating well while the rest were on a ration. I believed it was unfair and suggested that we stage a group protest to the boys. I talked to some other boys, and they were motivated to join in orchestrating the campaign.

We used A5 Sugar paper from the art room and got help from some house parents to make posters. We campaigned for ten minutes outside the school, shouting, "We are hungry; we want more food." The deputy head teacher demanded that we stop the protest, but we refused until it was agreed that the rations would be lifted. Finally, the deputy returned and said that the headmaster would meet with us, and three of us decided to meet him with our agenda. Throughout the session, the headmaster kept his eyes on me, letting me know I had organised the protest. I was glad we succeeded and convinced him to lift the rationing without conditions. The protest created a genuine sense of teamwork among the boys, and it was a collective effort that led to our success.

Anerley School 1971-1976

Chapter 13

My worse experience occurred when Duncan McAdam (1974) took over from Mr Ransom. McAdam verbally expressed openly in a packed class of mainly black boys, "I do not like black people, and for you to learn English, I suggest you read the newspaper". The Daily Mail paper was delivered to the school daily, and you could not get any more right-wing than that. I was speechless; I looked at him disgusted, as I thought education aimed to develop people and change bigoted ideas.

I joined McAdam's class expecting he had the required skills to teach and develop pupils' skills and distribute his knowledge to a broad audience not subjected to skin colour. In addition, I hoped to develop essential skills such as reading, speaking, listening, and writing from McAdam's teaching. His class population mostly comprised black boys, mostly boys from Africa, the Caribbean, and a few English males.

McAdam's classroom had the opportunity where excellent communication skills could have been developed because each pupil had a story to tell. But, sadly, McAdam's teaching style did not demand him to deliver a curriculum without prejudice, and he did not care whether we learned. Instead, he used the teaching and learning environment with a free pass to promote his racial hysteria, fully understanding that he could preach racism and get away with it; In the seventies, the UK was blighted by racism.

His attitude towards black people was unmistakably similar to the slave colonialists who treated black people below an unacceptable level of humanity. Moreover, his classroom environment was a breeding ground for intellectual stagnation; he offered no creative lessons that promoted stimulation of the mind for learners. McAdam had a negative approach, an approach I could not agree with.

So, instead, I took myself off to the village library and got some Teach-Yourself-English books. I wanted to learn the rules of language and how to speak and write efficiently within the host country.

I tried carrying out the exercises outlined in the book, copied the exercise tasks, and provided answers. But unfortunately, on one of the occasions, I got the tense wrong. Eric Milner, who was the woodwork teacher, an indolent man, spotted my mistake, and instead of pointing out the mistake, the error was made known to the staff team, teachers and house parents, as well as to his wife, who was not an employee of the school.

His wife, Betty Milner, mocked me incessantly with an insidious smirk and a sinister chuckle. Betty's smirk was a constant reminder of the racist dogma held by white people that education and the command of English were not designed for black people. In my four to five years in England, I learnt a lot. I overcome many fraught situations not to give into Betty's negativity and racist standpoint to affect my aspirations for self-improvement. On my next visit to the library, I asked the librarian if they were any English books with answers. I was handed one, and the instructions were challenging, but I could compare my answers.

I had sinus problems, which caused difficulty with breathing. McAdam inquired about what was wrong. I told him about difficulty with breathing, and I was directed to sniff Ammonia.

Next, he led me to the cleaning cupboard and advised me to transfer some Ammonia into a small bottle for personal use. I Followed McAdam's instructions, and surprisingly, after a few sniffs of the Ammonia, my nasal difficulties improved. On one occasion, whilst pouring Ammonia from the main bottle, Ron Nelson, a senior house parent, spotted what I was doing and asked questions.

Nelson confiscated the small plastic bottle and took me to the headmaster's office. I had no idea of the dangerous side effects of Ammonia until I was taken to the headmaster's office, where I was authoritatively told to stop sniffing the chemical because it could cause visual impairment, damage to my lungs, or death.

A lock was placed on the cleaning cupboard, and McAdam was called to the headmaster's office. I had no idea what was communicated to him. I did not have the required skill set to challenge or counter-challenge McAdam's acts of hateful racial objections against black people. I attended his class, not through choice but because there was no alternative. His appointed role was to teach English, but the teaching time was spent doing technical drawings. I tried to understand why his lessons focussed on techniques of technical drawings rather than English.

The majority of the teaching staff were more maladjusted than the pupils. I witnessed on numerous occasions that the headmaster and the woodwork teacher illegally took material that was supposed to be available for pupils for their purposes, such as building cabinets and tables, and charged the Inner London Education Authority. A neighbour of mine in Antigua gave me a rare

1925 threepence coin of King George 5th. I travelled with the coin from Antigua and had it until I commenced boarding school.

I gave the coin to Derek Lavirie for safekeeping; to the best of my recollection, Lavirie placed the coin in an envelope and put it in a locked cabinet in the staff room, which pupils never had access to staff rooms. I used to collect rare stamps as a hobby; Lavirie's stepson was also a stamp and coin collector. Invariably I used to ask Lavirie for the coin, and I would carry it around in my pocket for a day; the coin was used as a reminder of my good old days in Antigua.

After reminiscing about home, the coin was returned to Lavirie for safekeeping. On leaving boarding school, Lavirie gave me earth-shattering news when he stated, "I can't find the coin." I was devastated, and for a moment, I thought he was joking; I stood outside the staff room for at least five minutes, hoping that Lavirie would appear with the coin; unfortunately, he did not.

I left the school not knowing what to believe, was my coin lost genuinely, or was it deliberately stolen? The coin was significant and personal to me; a month after leaving the boarding school, I revisited and asked Lavirie if he had found the coin. He reacted aggressively and said, "I have already told you that the coin is lost; stop asking for it". I reflected on Lavirie's reaction; I felt disappointed and helpless as I was divested of a personal belonging that was a part of my journey to live in the UK.

The staff had little or no regard for black pupils; an example of their disregard towards black pupils was further demonstrated by the school's Domestic Bursar, who spotted a pupil and me engaging in chasing each other around the rose bed; she shouted at us, "Joe has just tidied those rose beds and not for you two nig nogs to destroy them". I was enraged, offended, and wanted to curse her, but I decided against it and reported her to the headmaster, who was her husband. He responded, "Don't notice what she said because she referred to our dog as a nig nog." I was unsure whom I was most exasperated with, the Domestic Bursar or the headmaster for equating us as dogs.

Racist slurs were prevalent in the school; my birth surname was O'Brien, and Eric Milner and others often referred to me as the "Black Paddy"; or "Sambo" Initially, I had no idea what a Paddy was. Duncan McAdam enjoyed giving his definition of a Paddy; he describes a Paddy as a "thick Irish man." He describes the Irish as ignorant thick peasants. I was perplexed by the constant reference to a "Black Paddy". I felt broken and mortified by the school's exhibit of racial abuse. My confidence and self-esteem were compromised. The racial slurs at the school contributed to changing my birth surname from O'Brien to Henry. The experience was a constant reminder of enslavement, where slaves had no rights, their identity was taken by force, and mine was violated through emotional and psychological abuse.

Racial name calling was not limited to the school environment, as I experienced racists slurs and acts of violence where white people would spit or throw water bombs followed by shouts of "Wogs go back home", "Sambo," "Nig Nogs f*** off out," at times it was unsafe to walk the streets of London out of fear of being attacked simply because of my skin colour. The vicious terms used against black people were unknown to me because, in Antigua, I was not exposed to racism. But, I was traumatised by the level of racism and hostility that were directed at black people in the "Motherland".

Night and Day-November 1975

If meeting my father for the first time and not under the influence of alcohol, he would come across as a jolly, amiable, and kind person. But, when he was under the influence of alcohol, he became, without reservation, a thoroughly different character, a remodelled character of being easy-going. But, unfortunately, his changed character would involve him being hazardously brutal. An example of his character change involved me having to fight for my life when I was fifteen years old.

My father came home on a Friday; it was about midnight, he was not staggeringly drunk, but the smell of alcohol was oozing out of his pores and breath; he called me and directed my attention to a bag with dirty laundry and requested that I take his brother's laundry to the launderette on Saturday morning and he left the money on the table in the passage. He and his wife were not on speaking terms for reasons unknown to me, she occupied the living room, and he remained in their matrimonial bedroom.

On a Saturday morning, I got up to take the clothes to the laundrette as was directed; my mother asked, "Where are you going?" I said, "Daddy asked me to take Uncle Shirley's clothes to the launderette." She said, "No, leave them right there" I was confused, knowing that I was dammed if I did and dammed if I didn't; I opted for the latter. I wondered all day why my mother would deliberately put me in an awkward position, as she was very well aware of the living situation that was already turbulent, and no doubt her directions to disobey his instructions deliberately would only cause a volcanic eruption.

The Saturday night, he came home and found the bag of soiled clothes in the same position he had left them with the money on the table. He entered the bedroom I shared with my brother to determine why I had not carried the clothes to the launderette. He was inebriated, or at least under the influence of alcohol, which was not unusual for him on a Saturday night. I told him what my mother had instructed me to do. His temperament changed to a thunderous rage; he left the bedroom, returned with a paraffin heater, opened the paraffin tank, and doused me with paraffin.

He stood by the bedroom door; I watched his actions with horror and fear for my life; I felt trapped, as the apartment was on the fifth floor. Then, he took out his lighter to set me alight. Fortunately, the council worked in the bedroom, and a workman left a stick. I grabbed the stick, and I was able to beat the lighter out of his hand as the lighter dropped; luckily, he was too drunk to search for it; he left the bedroom and went to the kitchen to look for the chef's knife but returned with a meat fork. His eyes were blood shots and overflowing with fury, and his arms were flailing like a madman. The folk was being aimed for my throat; I dodged the swings made by the folk before deciding that it was him or I. I swung a blow aiming to knock the folk out of his hand, and the folk dropped at that point; my mother came to the bedroom and engendered a human wall between him and me; she said, "Go to Vaney."

I ran out of the apartment in my underwear; as I got outside the flat, my mother shouted out of the window and threw some clothes outside. Vaney is my brother's godmother. I quickly put on the clothes that were thrown outside. I ran as fast as I could. I was not sure if he was coming after me or not. I have no recollection of how I got to Vaney's abode because, in 1974, there were no night buses, and all other forms of transport stopped running at midnight. I ran from Pimlico to Paddington and arrived at Vaney's abode, frightened, distressed, and traumatised from the incident where I had to fight for my life and escape a potentially explosive situation for my life. I stayed at Vaney's abode until Sunday afternoon and returned to boarding school.

Paraffin Heater

Meat Fork

Chapter 14

Admission into Care

I returned to boarding school on Sunday evening, shell-shocked from what occurred on Saturday night; I searched my mind for answers and cogitated what wrong I had committed for coming close to losing my life. My father had committed a heinous offence against me for wrongdoing that I did not commit. My mother knowingly put me in an impossible situation. Whatever their argument was about, I ended up bearing the brunt of it to the point it almost cost me my life. However, I am inclined to believe that she did not expect him to douse me with paraffin to set me alight or to stab me with the meat fork, but perhaps I would have got a good flogging.

I remembered arriving at school in a distraught state, but I reframed from discussing with anyone what had transpired over the weekend. I was still struggling to understand how I might have contributed to have caused him to try to kill me; furthermore, I did not know who I could talk with, and there was the fear that talking about the incident might have made matters worse for me, so I continued to suffer in silence. Finally, on Thursday during the week of returning to school, I was called to the headmaster's office, where I was told I had to attend Westminster Social Service Office. I was given no further information and did not ask for what purpose.

I arrived at the social service office in Victoria, where a male introduced himself as a Social Worker. Before meeting the social worker, I had never come in contact with one in my entire life; I was not even aware of the role of a social worker. He said my mother had contacted social services, and the authority agreed to admit me into care. I was never interviewed by Westminster Social Services to obtain my views. I went along with the brief conversation with the social worker. The reason for placing me into care was never made known. In those days, the voice of the child was not heard. I had yet to learn what he was talking about. Looking back, I was severely disadvantaged by Westminster Social Services; they failed to obtain my views but accepted a one-sided account. The social worker did not ask for my version of the event, and I did not volunteer. He did not tell me the story my mother gave to social services, but her narration was sufficiently convincing for admission into care to have agreed. I was taken to a children's home in Burnham Beeches, Slough. Upon arriving at the house, we were met by the Officer in Charge; the OIC was amiable. The social worker left, and the OIC gave me an induction of the abode, which housed two children, but I was the only one for at least three to four weeks.

I was shown to my room; after that, she offered a cup of tea, and we sat and chatted. As I narrated my story, my voice was listened to. Still, my account was in-depth, dated to being taken from my abode, where I wander freely, loved and cared for. I opened up to the OIC and told her what caused me to end up in social services accommodations. The OIC appeared dumbfounded as I told her what I had to do to escape being almost set on fire or stabbed. It was assumed from her facial expressions of puzzlement that my story differed from what was told to social services. I found the new environment to be whacky, and I was an alien placed in an environment that was new and exposed to a culture different from my Antiguan way of life.

I spent the night in a new environment, living with strangers, and once again, my time was spent wondering what I did wrong to end up where I was. I lay in the room's darkness; the environment was quiet and, in an outlandish way, very peaceful. I reflected on the events that caused me to be where I was. The experience resulted from what had occurred with the man who was supposed to be my father, who tried to kill me; it was hard for me to come to terms with the events, and I was overcome by it all. I felt frightened as I was alone with my thoughts; I could not find answers to the many whys. I was all alone; I was unnoticeably burdened by the bundle of traumas imposed by others.

I spent eight months in the care of Westminster Social Services, which was contrastingly different from being in the care of my grandmother, sisters, and nannies. Still, nonetheless, I settled for what was available, as the desirable was out of my reach. Throughout the time spent in Westminster Care, my parents made no efforts to get in touch through letters, cards, phone calls, or visits; history repeated itself. So, I wondered why I came to the "Motherland" to end up in social services care. Still, in retrospect, it was a better and safer alternative than being deliberately placed in an unjustifiable position where ultimately, I had to fight my way out of a dangerous and life-threatening situation.

The trauma I had endured from being placed in social services care was equal to the enslaved people who were removed from their homeland by brutal force. I never had a say in the process of being put into care. For years I carried the mental pain resulting from the physical and mental traumas; it all seemed unreal, but I kept going on.

Chapter 15

Bereavement

My late grandmother and other family members of her generation were born in Gunthrope Village Osborn, St George, in May 1900; they were brutally evicted from their hamlets by the Americans in 1942 and moved to NewWinthropes Village.

My beloved grandmother died at age seventy-five, twenty-two days after her birthday. I was fourteen and a half when I got the news. My belly sunk to rock bottom at the news of her passing away. In an instant, I experienced the pain I had never experienced. The person who cared for and nurtured me from seven months to age ten was no more. I experienced depression and anxiety. I had no one to talk with or share my grief with, so I suffered in silence until; eventually, I could pull myself together and focus on the good memories. Forty-eight years on, I still miss her and shed tears, but my tears are ones of gratefulness.

She raised my four sisters and me without ever complaining. She made good with the life that was given to her. My grandfather died when my mother was one-year-old, so my sisters and I grew up in a sole-parent household. She was a tough lady with a heart of a gladiator, a no-nonsense person. My grandmother was a person who never gave up; she kept on going even when the going got tough. She was full of compassion, giving, and kind-hearted. She was prominent throughout our community and was fondly called Aunt Mem or Cousin Mem. My grandmother navigated my childhood, as well as my entire life. She was my representation, a paradigm of strength; her steadfastness and forthrightness inspired me.

RIP

Unanswered questions

My father's alcoholism and impulsive temperament denied me the opportunity to get acquainted with who he was and what he thought of me. He has never told me that he loved me or has taken an interest in my feelings, and he has never inquired about my future ambitions. I was denied knowing the significant role of a father-son relationship. I have never understood why he supported or concurred with removing me from the life I had in Antigua, as he has never contributed positively to making life better for me in the UK.

He had three brothers in the UK, but they were unimportant in my life. As a result, I grew up lacking trust towards men, especially as I did not know whether I would be exposing myself to further pain, as I had encountered from my father. Under those circumstances, I found it challenging to form social links with men, with family or friends, because, from an early age, the main root of deference, bond, and trust was broken from being exposed to my father.

I have endeavoured to stop giving him a wide berth, being exasperated or caustic towards him. I was opportune on 31st August 1997 to spend some time with him, although he was in a coma; I held his hand and apologised for not getting acquainted before he departed Planet Earth. I did a generic eulogy; given the circumstances, that was the best I could have done for him. But, unfortunately, I could not express my true inner feelings, which were utter contempt, nor vent any emotional feelings, no tears because there were none to shed. They had long been washed away over time.

I am sure, but there must have been good reasons for his excessive drinking habits; he lived through Colonialisation and Windrush, and the two oppressive systems would have affected his mental well-being. However, I can only assume he decided by being taken in by the false news spread throughout the Caribbean.

'The Motherland needs you'; he answered the call to come to the UK under the misguided impression that he would contribute to rebuilding the UK and creating a better life for himself. But, discovering what he had expected and encountered did not measure up. Consequently, the disappointments, hostility, and racism he experienced may have contributed to his mental wellness and, ultimately, his family life.

Chapter 16

Bullying Tactics

The people of the Caribbean have been subjected to separation and loss throughout history. In the past, the area now known as "Coolidge" airport was called "Winthorpe Village" and was home to prime real estate. The land was owned by various families, including the Camachos, McDonald's, and Gomes. The village of High Point was even the site of the main runway. When the British leased Winthorpe Village to the Americans, they received fifty outdated destroyers in exchange for a ninety-nine-year lease on the land.

This leasing arrangement has similarities to how the British viewed Antiguans as easy targets. Leasing Winthorpe Village allowed the Americans easy access and protected their South Coast from "enemies." They were interested in Judges Bay, Millar, Crabbs, Highpoint, Coolidge, and the surrounding areas.

Initially, the villagers resisted leaving their homes despite the Americans' promises of a well-planned village with proper infrastructure. Instead, they suggested the Americans look for an alternative location. Finally, under duress, the elders agreed that negotiating with the government was in their best interest.

The villagers demonstrated a formidable front; consequently, the Americans became irritated by the delays and keen to progress with their project; they tried violent and churlish tactics by bulldozing villagers' homes and limiting the development of their crops. The Americans bulldozed their homes and created a scene akin to a fire inferno by setting fire to them, releasing the villagers' livestock from their pens, and destroying cooking utensils, instilling fear in them.

The villagers' lives were destroyed due to the Americans' actions. Northern villagers were also imprisoned on their land and country. However, villagers, including children, were given a pass to show when leaving and returning to their hamlet. Mary G Quinn (n.d.) said. "We were prisoners in our own country."

The Americans were resolute that villagers had to leave but agreed to let the Macdonald's remain. The reported purpose was that they were elderly and infirm, blind, and his wife had hearing impediments; they were white, and Antigua's planter's class was indeed an additional factor.

Social life for the MacDonald and numerous other white families rapidly included the American officers. One of MacDonald's daughters married an American officer.

Under duress, the villagers finally agreed to relocate. Were the Americans responsible for genocide after the American invasion by evicting the villagers from their homes? Mass graves were dug in the bushes at the runway's end. The area was surrounded by iron fencing, but it is unknown if the bodies are still there or if they have been moved to unknown locations.

The Americans signed a leasing agreement for the Northern village in 1941, and their work began that day. Although the overall lease agreement was delayed until March 1941, the Americans raised their flag on March 1941, but work on the Navy base had been underway since February 1941. The first United States Armed Forces members, consisting of fifty marines, started working on the sites in March 1941.

The actions of the Americans were equal to the middle passage, in which West Africans were forcibly removed from their homeland and transported to an unknown destination. The issue became where to transfer them to. The Anglican clergy at St. George's Church did not want to lose a big part of his congregation who recommended Fitches Creek, but the villagers argued that it was too swampy. The government's negotiators recommended moving to other parts of the island, but the villagers were firm that they were "Northerners" and wanted to remain in the north.

Acceptably four villages were formed, and NewWinthropes was agreed as the new name, followed by Barnes Hill, Piggotts and Cedar Grove. The imposed eviction separated family and kinship. My ancestors decided to relocate west of Barnes Hill. The American compensation package was repulsive and despicable in comparison to natural equity.

The Americans agreed to improve basic infrastructure, such as water, electricity, and sanitation, and build new homes for evacuees. They did construct some new homes, such as the Hampson, whose senior Hampson was a village elder. Despite this, many villagers were displaced, and the model village never materialised.

Hampson's house, courtesy of the Americans

The Americans paid the British an undisclosed compensatory package to design NewWinthropes as a model village. However, the British Administration took the money and reneged on the agreement. As a result, they are original NewWinthropenans who are still living without direct water to their homes, are still using latrines and with poor sanitation. The parliamentary representative for NewWinthropes is expected to call on the British to fulfil the agreement between them and the Americans, complete the house-building project, and improve sanitation and infrastructure, which was agreed upon in 1941.

Furthermore, the value of property in NewWinthropes is not equal to the value of the property from which they were forcibly evicted, as properties in Coolidge and the surrounding areas are worth significantly more.

Antigua's history, American base. Picture taken from Life magazine.

In my village, after emancipation from slavery and pre-colonialism, bartering was the way of life for many people. It was a relatively cash-free community where people traded goods; for example, a farmer may exchange yam for meat. The traders would discuss and negotiate the magnitude of yam in exchange. For the transaction to go ahead, it was subjected to the quality of the items and the agreed amount. Bartering was influential in our small community; people revered each other. Interchanging things worked within our village because it was a small and not affluent community, but everyone knew each other well. The barter economy within us sanctioned the individual traders to strive and demonstrate their flair. The bartering economy within our village shows that communities could benefit from personal skills. Unique skills, flair and integrity demanded individual traders to develop their expertise, which helped the community as a whole.

Items that a particular trader did not need were purchased to enable them to barter to trade for things necessary to their desire. Bartering was not restricted to buying food items, as villagers had other skills such as dressmaking, cooking, carpentry, shoe repair, hair styling and fishing. The village's primary income sources were agriculture and ground provision. Our village population needed to be more significant for anyone to work full-time.

The effect of society and community evolving impacted the bartering economy, as communities could carry their goods into town, where they were exposed to a money economy and often had no awareness of their buyers. Still, some people needed their goods or services. Because of the changes in bartering within the community, food for assistance has been eradicated, as well as close-kitted communities where people know each other. There was no differentiation between the community population. Furthermore, the changes to a money society made it obligatory for traders to equip themselves with marketable skills to meet the demands of the new style of trading, e.g. shoe repairs and carpentry, which was subjected to specific customers' needs.

The island's economy was exporting raw materials to the first world and importing finished goods to be consumed by residents. The island also heavily relied upon credit from Western banks like Barclays, which was often prejudicial in the lending along the line of race; ironically, the initial capital for the Barclays bank came from the slave trade. The local economy was dominated by foreign traders from the Middle East and politicians who owned or held a stake in every significant business in the country. Thus, despite being independent, the local populace, in a genuine sense, was economically enslaved. Outside of a few wealthy and elite businessmen and politicians, there was little wealth in the hands of the population. Through tourism, the local population remained dependent on white foreigners for most of their income.

Antigua's economy centred on trading raw materials to the so-called developed countries, and the top items were sold to locals in Antigua. Despite what preceded Antigua, which relied substantially upon obtaining credit from Western banks, for example, Barclays was usually prejudiced in lending to Antigua. Migrant traders from Syria and Lebanon, including local politicians, monopolise Antigua's economy.

In Antigua, the local economy is mainly dominated by migrant traders from the Middle East and politicians who have a financial interest in significant businesses. Although it is an independent country, the native citizens have been economically oppressed and have limited wealth, with only a small group of successful business people and politicians holding significant wealth. Nonetheless, tourism was the only option for most of the population to evade the poverty trap, causing them to rely on white foreigners for their income. Antiguans' identity and history have been unavoidably entangled with colonialism and tourism. Our unscrupulous politicians and the corruption left behind by the colonisers upon their departure from Antigua accommodated the infringement of iniquities.

Profiteering and colonisation are inextricably linked; why is there a follow-on with oppression? The differentiation of classism was the norm during colonial days and caused an unchanging system. The British would have us believe its system was designed to avail us, but in reality, its approach was harvesting more out of us than it was contributing. Antigua's political regime was operating whorehouses, mismanagement of public funds and being part of unscrupulous transactions.

There is no opposition from the people because they were conditioned and influenced into being compliant and unassertive causes of history. The class differences designed by crookedness and colonisation tie in with having prejudiced perceptions of black people as aliens. Those well-off in the regime did not see they were blameworthy as they always gained from the poor socio-economical people and did not care about the consequences.

The "poor" and grovelers" go hand in hand. The system does not cater to voiceless individuals or those who cannot influence the economic market. The voiceless of society perpetuate to be unheard and exploited through drugs, frugal labour and prostitution. Changes for those individuals remain unchallenged, and perpetual oppression becomes the norm.

However, some of our forefathers were strong-willed people with strong voices who worked tirelessly to build our country. They exhibited the tenacity of Hercules Pillar by withstanding storms. They were skilled in many areas such as agriculture, also known as negro ground, fishing, cooking, and pottery craft work, all of which were required skills for the construction of our nation. Men were the household patriarchs, and they were responsible for providing for their families. Furthermore, women were housewives who stayed at home to care for their children, but women were not limited to the role of a 'housewife.'

Antiguans were known for their ability to save money and their dedication to education. Antigua even helped develop the education and religious systems of other Leeward islands. This dedication to progress stemmed from recognising that Antigua needed to rebuild after being ravaged by colonialism. In the past, Antiguans would keep their savings at home until they had enough to deposit in a bank. Some even went to great lengths to keep their money safe, such as tying it up in handkerchiefs, bras, straw beds, or pillows and burying it in a specific location.

The independence of Antigua and Barbuda was not the result of international pressure on colonialists who had oppressed the indigenous Afro-Antiguans for centuries. The British left on their own terms. The transfer of power from the British to the people of Antigua and Barbuda was not violent as in other jurisdictions under its control, possibly because Antiguans and Barbudans did not present themselves as an unswerving group of people seeking endless war. Still, we had a voice that did not directly threaten the British.

Hercules Pillars- Galleon Bay Antigua

Chapter 17

Empires

The British and Americans brought enslaved and forced labour to the Caribbean shores to establish prosperous cities in America, the UK and other European countries. This also extended the British and other European Empires. The Americans introduced racism to Antigua more than ever, promoting race awareness, racial bigotry, and spite.

Although racism was not new to Antiguans, the middle class still faced hidden and open colour obstacles. At the same time, those from a working-class background who travelled to America and the UK and served in the UK armed forces during World War two returned home outraged about their experiences with discrimination.

Marcus Garvey was a significant figure in promoting Black Nationalism across the Caribbean. His ideas had a profound impact, leading to the establishment of trade unions, political parties, and cultural institutions. Garvey believed the black Caribbean could overcome racism by having confidence in themselves and avoiding defeat. As a result, his followers were motivated to work towards self-governance and the advancement of their communities. Marcus Garvey's movement helped sharpen the understanding of racism in Antigua and the Caribbean region.

There was a time when black Americans could not vote, own property, or enter certain professions such as teaching or medicine. They were forced to live in segregated neighbourhoods and attend inferior schools with separate facilities for white and black children, such as white and black toilets and canteens. Segregation was enshrined in Caribbean people, which dates back to the Middle Passage era, where children were dragged from their mothers, and tribes were separated and shipped out to different lands. Black people were not born as a conquered race but as free people. The Europeans imposed their ideas of civilisation on the captured slave. Although these policies have slowly been abolished, racism continues to exist today.

During the first Century BC, the Europeans introduced the 'Empire'; the rationale for its introduction was to describe 'civilisation' and not a command. The Europeans endeavour to establish empires in different parts of the world. The prosperity of an empire varied in that while others were outstanding, others were only temporary. To a significant extent, the wealth of the European empires depended upon the coloniser's competency to adjust to and control the natural environment that they encountered.

For the Europeans to acquire lands that did not belong to them, they had to understand the environment to take control. It was through understanding the environment that they were able to take control. The British colonisers could assert their influence and govern the people in the new lands by taking power. An example of lasting domination was the British Empire because they understood the 'natural environment,' which allowed them to expand significantly. Initially, the British were weary of the Mughal control of power, so they took essential steps to avoid conflict with the Mughal Empire demonstrating their understanding of the 'natural environment.'

The British obtained authority from the Mughals to establish a trading business. However, when the power and dominance of the Mughal sovereignty and authority commenced dwindling, the British seized the opportunity, gradually acquired the right of governorship, and introduced taxation to the region. The approach gave them notability and a prosperous and robust authority in South Asia.

Many studies have clarified the function of Kingdoms, showing that control within them can occur based on purposes rather than force or an accumulation of the two. It can be exercised through various military and economic manipulation, as demonstrated by the British in India and cultural exhibits. It can be formal or informal to flowing degrees. The designation of characteristics and people in the outer region of the Kingdom can differ considerably.

Some players from the outer region can access the decision-making process and resources from the administrative sovereignty within the chief town or sovereign domination; on the other hand, some were unable to access resources, so they were kept out at times and encountered discrimination, hostility, and exploration. The relationship between administrative sovereignty and players was categorised, and conflict was unavoidably ordained. However, democratic empires were confirmed by less oppressive rulership.

Different Kingdoms have emerged throughout history in various ways. Some have achieved sovereignty by stabilising neighbouring areas or attempting to convert their inhabitants to a particular religion. Others have emerged through modernisation and social differentiation. It's important to note that a sovereign state doesn't necessarily come into existence through aggression. Each

Kingdom has unique characteristics and has caused different outcomes based on its historical era.

Alexander the Great, for example, built his Kingdom using military force, while the Roman Empire relied more on language and law to unify its people. The Chinese Han Empire was known for its administrative skills, while the British, French, Portuguese, and Spanish Empires used their maritime power for trading. The Soviet Empire employed idealistic outlets alongside military, political, and economic techniques to build its Empire.

Unfortunately, black people are often stereotyped as lazy and criminals. The government accepted these behaviours in Antigua, which dismayed many Antiguans and Barbudans and disgusted Magnet (December 20, 1943). However, the UK government allowed local political administrations to manage such matters. For instance, when a Kittian complainant reported that Americans only allowed whites into "places of refreshments," the Colonial Secretary refuted this. In one example, the Colonial Office informed a British member of parliament that the matter would be left to the local government and administration.

It's important to note that each Kingdom and government has unique challenges and methods of dealing with them. For example, a worker from Antigua at the airbase shared his initial experience there. He noticed toilet signs labelled "white" and "black," which made him unsure which one to use since he did not fit into either category. As a result, he resorted to using the woods instead.

Racism in America was fierce and personal, with obscene utterances, sloshed road hogs, dustups, fracases and regular shootouts. The American soldiers expected Antiguan employees to obey their orders, and they resorted to verbal abuse and physical violence. They were macho and aggressive and predisposed to producing guns and knives. Several threatening incidents resulted in deaths. For example, a local known as Son-Son was shot by a Marine in town after refusing to obey orders.

It was not the colour of our skin that they were terrified of. Instead, it was our fortified prowess, morals and cultural values that they strived to break by imposing their educational system and cultural and religious systems that subsequently enslaved us; Caribbeans are dominated and influenced by the Americans, British and European cultural values. We are conditioned to think that their values are superior.

It has, however, been widely acknowledged that slavery was an appalling act against humanity. Contrastingly, after the Second World War, the Jews were paid one hundred and forty million US Dollars for five years for their enslavement which affirmed that white people would stand with white people. Black people are the only race that will stand against their race to subjugate their race with being oppressed.

Unfortunately, black leaders have not learnt lessons from our chiefs that sold fellow Africans into slavery. The chiefs thought they were benefitting until the European colonialists realised the chiefs' level of nativity and colonised us on our continent. They also colonised those chiefs who lost everything gained from backstabbing their people.

Prince Klass, Antigua's first national hero, was betrayed by his fellow Africans. Klass devised a plot to overthrow the Colonialists. He shared his ideas with his fellow Africans, who informed the colonialists, causing Klass to die brutally and preventing Antigua from becoming the first liberated state in the Caribbean. Additionally, no African country has apologised to the Caribbean people for their contributions during the slave trade era.

In 1625, Barbados became the first island to be possessed by the British Empire. After that, the British Empire colonised other islands in the region. The islands were regarded as gainfully and financially rewarding, perfect assets for the Empire. White Gold was the major money-making asset for the Empire.

No Compensation

The White Gold was cultivated, germinated, and prepared for transportation to the UK. As a result, the Middle Passage slave trade was the topmost trafficking of people that has ever evolved in human history. Within a short time, the colonised islands became environments for misemployment, physical abuse, and torture.

The islands became the epicentre, where West African slaves were plunged into coerced labour and bankrolled the British Empire's industrial revolution. A massive range of luxury was brought from the slaves' labour. Many UK cities such as London, Bristol, Cardiff and Liverpool flourished immensely. These cities flourished in abundant affluence from free labour gained from slaves' involuntary labour, and the British Empire grew.

Coerced enslavement ended in 1833; the slaves' owners were financially made good for their losses, more than twenty thousand pounds, and the slaves that ploughed the cane fields received no compensation for their labour. As a result, the Caribbean colonies became a melting pot for all races; the Caribbean basin was the united nations for oppressed people, especially the white British working classes, the Iberian Jews, the Middle East, and labourers from India and China, the Caribbean became a combined nation for oppressed people.

Some of the non-African races that subsisted in the Caribbean were regarded as Octoroon, Mulatto, and Quadroon. Albeit slavery was officially abolished, the British plantocracy maintained an apartheid system that they triumphed over; the divide-and-rule stance was maintained throughout the Caribbean.

The Caribbean apartheid system occurred approximately four thousand miles from the Motherland, which made it possible for the atrocities committed by the British to be erased from recollection as if they had never happened. Much has been said about the American slaves more than the British slaves. There is very little information documented about what life was like for the British slaves; there is no mention of mental health issues that the British slaves endured, their suffering under the British Empire, and what life was like for those enslaved individuals without a voice. Black Caribbean decedents from West Africa have long been denied the opportunity of having their voices heard. The undefined inheritance passed down to generations from the British Slave Empire remains vague, as oppression, murder, rape, deception, disconnecting and disunion of black people from their homeland and subjugating them into coerced labour and cheap labour cannot be all that defines us.

Chapter 18

When will we ever learn?

Following the Second World War, the UK government invited Caribbeans to come and help rebuild the country. Churchill had previously asked white Commonwealth citizens to stay and contribute to rebuilding, but this was unsuccessful. So, British recruiters went to the Caribbean and used emotive language to encourage people to move to the UK, promising employment in various sectors.

Most of those who came to the UK were men who had previously held good jobs in their homeland and had excellent references. They were confident they would be welcomed in the "Motherland", especially since the UK Nationality Act of that year offered British status to former colonial citizens.

However, despite the need for workers, the Guardian 1968 (n.d) reported that the British Monarchy did not appoint "coloured" immigrants or foreigners to clerical roles in the Royal household. The Caribbeans' invitees arrived in the UK on the Empire Windrush on June 22, 1948, and disembarked at Tilbury Docks. Around four hundred and ninety-two invitees arrived, many of whom were veterans of World War two. They came intending to find employment and contribute to rebuilding their homeland.

Arrival of invitees

Throughout history, the British Empire had a long murderous history of executing their endeavours by building their Empire by claiming lands, assets and coerced and frugal labour. The British colonialists invaded the Asante Kingdom; they carried out grotesque wrongdoings against humanity, seized artefacts, and ultimately 1874, burned down the Manhyia Stone Palace. Finally, the

British Annexed the Asante Kingdom, causing the King and others to flee into exile to Seychelles.

The Windrush generations and their decedents can attest to the same experiences of the atrocities inflicted on them, hash encounters of physical and outburst, isolation, and separations, which dates back to the cruel British acts against humanity that have been left with generations. Windrush generations and decedents experience nights of fearfulness, despair, and lethargy. They had to endure impediments by being treated less than second-class citizens in the land that was supposed to be their "Motherland."

There are many of the same attributes between the Windrush era and the Caribbean service women men who answered the call to join the British service men and women to fight against Hitler and rebuild the UK. There was widespread enthusiasm throughout the Caribbean for Caribbean men and women to join forces with the British servicemen and women to defend the King and the Empire and defeat Nazis Germany.

The Caribbean service men and women who answered the "call" to accommodate the King and defend the Empire made significant contributions and sacrifices for the fall of Nazism and the promotion of "democracy." Still, they got insufficient apperceptions for their efforts in monetary terms or from the King. Once the war was over, the Caribbeans who sacrificed so much to make Britain "great" efforts were forgotten; they were no longer regarded as "British" citizens but were treated like aliens, harshly and plagued by racist abuse and virtually forgotten.

Many Caribbean people believed England was their "Motherland", and Caribbean schoolchildren were taught to view themselves as British citizens. However, their prospects and dreams about the "Motherland" in less than no time became a myth resulting from the cold reception they had received upon arriving in the UK. Eleven Labour MPs opposed staging their objections to the UK Prime Minster Attlee that the admittance of the invitees "coloured" people would impact the way of life of the white British population.

Many talks have been made about the British "Motherland," but what does it mean? The invitees experienced a hostile environment, aggressiveness, racism and alienation, mental health, depression, and rejections in finding employment and housing; many of the invitees experienced homelessness living in halfway housing and having no entitlements to public funds. Consequently, they had no choice but to accept their lot. After all, they were not considered invitees but immigrants.

They took steps to avoid conflicts with the host citizens of the "Mother" country. The invitees endeavoured to fit in with the host country's citizens, the "Motherland", to the point where some stopped speaking their Creole language and were ashamed of their native Creole language. The Creole language has been around far longer than "Standard English," more commonly known as "Queen's English." They came with the prospect that they would be treated as equals with the host's citizens, but that assumed view became a nightmare from hell for many.

There is a range of languages spoken in Caribbean islands, like many facets of our culture, which have been a direct result of our history. The spoken language in the Caribbean came from our enslaved history and was determined by our colonial monarchs, England, Spain, France, Portugal, and Holland. The primary spoken language was French Creole, English Creole, Papiamentu, and Saramccan. Wrongly, the Creole language is on the brink of being stopped while Standard English is revered, albeit Creole has been around far longer than Standard English. English has taken centre stage through Cyber land, multimedia, social networks, music, television, and businesses operating in other countries.

English has gained popularity in many African countries, particularly in West Africa, and is also spoken in the Caribbean. This could be because Standard English is commonly used in Western advertising, movies, and music and is associated with the West idea of prosperity. Unfortunately, as more people use English, other lesser-known languages, including Creole languages, are disappearing. This is due to the influence of globalisation, multimedia, and technology, which have contributed to the disappearance, and it is essential to note that when languages are lost, so are the associated cultural traditions.

The Caribbean is a hub for numerous religious and non-religious celebrations, each with its distinctive feature to enjoy. Celebrations are an essential part of Caribbean culture, showcasing the rich history and diversity of the region. These events also allow entrepreneurs to market their products and promote cultural expressions in a positive and uplifting environment. There are, however, countless celebrations that are observed throughout the Caribbean. The celebration could be religious or non-religious. There is always something distinctive to appreciate from experience within the islands. Celebrations are very paramount to the Caribbeans. Unique celebrations reflect the rich cultural diversity and history of the Caribbean basin. Celebrations are seen as inspiring prospects for entrepreneurs to market their products and, at the same time, allow them to demonstrate a range of cultural expressions.

Christmas celebrations, such as Christmas Carols, tourism, Antigua's sailing week, Antigua's Carnival, and arts and crafts designed for the tourist market. The presence of

Western celebrities and media outlets is very apparent and undebatable, making it arduous for locals.

As a Caribbean individual, it can be challenging to establish a network that includes Western countries due to limited financial resources, lack of access to influential contacts and visa restrictions. While many Caribbean Islands are independent, their residents face challenges in progressing internationally because of unequal opportunities in global markets. This can hinder the ability of young Caribbean entrepreneurs to showcase their skills and talents as independent individuals.

There are religious holidays and events like 'Good Friday,' Easter Sunday, and Christmas during celebrations. However, Christmas has become more of a consumer holiday, losing sight of the true meaning behind the event. In addition, the capitalist ideas promoted by Western society have influenced the Caribbean, resulting in a need for more appreciation for religious affairs. Antigua was a joyful and exciting place during Christmas, where families gathered to exchange gifts and enjoy traditional Christmas drinks like Sorrel and Ginger beer.

Being surrounded by loved ones, eating and drinking together was heart-warming. However, my experience in the UK with my parents was different. Although my mother tried her best to bring my brother and me together for a Christmas meal without my father, his unpredictable behaviour made his absence unsettling. He never participated in any gatherings or special occasions with us. He always seemed to crave attention, especially when he was drunk. Sadly, my parents never gave my brother or me a Christmas gift. I cannot speak for my brother's experiences before he turned seven, as I wasn't present then.

While living with my parents, I didn't enjoy the holiday season much, despite my love for vintage Christmas carols like Silent Night and I Saw Three Ships. However, after becoming a single parent, I ensured my son had a great Christmas every year. We always had a Christmas tree with lights, and he loved decorating it, especially eating the chocolate ornaments. I involved him in preparing the Christmas feast and all the traditional trimmings, even though I secretly disliked the holiday season.

I have never been fond of the saying, "I'm dreaming of a white Christmas." Living with Mr Grinch for so long had made me feel down about the holiday season. It did not feel like a festive and warm occasion, especially when you are far away from loved ones who made Christmas special. There was nothing white about it.

Chapter 19

Employment & Discrimination

I finished compulsory education in 1976 and secured a place on a pre-vocational course at Brixton College. Before starting the course, I needed to find a job. I went to the Job Centre on Edgware Road, and while browsing job sections, I noticed a job vacancy for an Office Junior at the British Plastic Federation that paid £25.00 per week. I presented the ad ticket to the receptionist, who contacted the employer to confirm the position was still open. The employer confirmed it was, but the employer asked if I was black in a discreet manner.

The receptionist was unsettled by the covert question and answered, "Yes". The receptionist confirmed that the position was no longer available, but when I returned to the Job Centre a week later, I saw that the job was still being advertised. At first, I thought about reapplying, but it became clear that I was rejected because of my skin colour. This experience showed that black Caribbeans weren't given the same opportunities as others in the "Motherland". All sense of fairness and humanity had been taken away.

To maintain my independence, I had an urgent need for a job. I decided to check out the job board at the employment centre, where I found a job listing for a Linen Porter position at the Stratford Court Hotel on Oxford Street. I applied for the job, and the Housekeeper invited me for an interview. Fortunately, I was offered a full-time job as a Linen Porter and worked there until September 1976. Later, I switched to a part-time schedule of only two days per week, Saturdays and Sundays, to pursue my full-time course.

The position as a Linen Porter was demanding work, back aching. I dragged, distributed, and collected soiled linen from all floors, the hours were long, and the wages were small but adequate to live on from week to week, though not extravagantly. The work was reminiscent of black- labourers harvesting White Gold trying to advance the British Empire's economy. Racism, despite anti-racist and discrimination laws, is not a bygone period in British history as it is still very active in all areas of life in the UK.

Despite having qualifications, Caribbeans who lived and arrived in Britain often faced discrimination from employers who only offered them low-paying jobs in areas that native citizens deemed beneath them, such as cleaning and manual labour. While some were fortunate to find work, many were left without job opportunities.

In the workplace, black individuals often encounter additional obstacles and must put in double the effort compared to their white colleagues. I have faced racial discrimination throughout my career in education. However, in 2008, while working as the only hourly paid black male staff member in the English department at a further education college, I hold a MA in Education, a Cert in Education and ten years of experience teaching Post Compulsory Learners.

I responded to a job opening for a full-time English lecturer in the English department. I completed the application process and participated in an interview, but I did not receive any updates from the Human Resources Department for two months. I thought that I was not chosen for the position. However, I was taken aback when I met the newly appointed person in the hallway and learned that she got the job. She was a white female with no teaching experience or educational qualifications and had previously worked as additional learning support staff. While congratulating her, I was disappointed that the college did not inform me of their decision. It felt like a case of covert racism and sexism, which is discouraging in this day and age. I did not address the situation.

I am aware that proving covert discrimination can be challenging and time-consuming. Whilst working in another Further Education in Hertfordshire as an Early Years Coordinator. I was the only black male member of the staff team. I came up against covert racism, bullying and sexual harassment. Following my appointment, I emailed my line manager requesting a syllabus for the Level 2 Diploma in Early Years Education programme.

Although I was waiting to hear from my line manager, I proactively developed my Scheme of Work using the syllabus provided by the External Examining Board. After two months, I was summoned to the Deputy Dean's office, where I was informed that my line manager had reported me for teaching without a Scheme of Work. I became perplexed when I emailed my line manager to request the course syllabus but received no response. Consequently, I created my syllabus. Later, the Dean became aware of the situation and requested to inspect the email I sent to my line manager. Upon reviewing it alongside the examining board syllabus, the Dean appeared humbled and commended me for being proactive. She instructed me always to make sure I cover my back.

The faculty head for Early Years and Education was an elderly white Dutch female who tended to hug and rub her front on mine, followed by "Come on, William, let's have some sexual harassment". Her sexual overtures were highly offensive and inappropriate. The second time the Head of Faculty attempted to fulfil her exotic fantasy, she was stopped and told, "I am a professional, and my brains are not in my boxer's shorts."

Following my objections to being sexually violated, I constantly faced unjustified attacks from colleagues; going to work each morning was like meeting the St. Trinians' without the Hockey Sticks. Undoubtedly, if a black man were to have conducted himself in the manner that the Faculty Head of the Department displayed, he would have been charged with Gross Misconduct.

Chapter 20

Racism and Education

1998 I registered for a Master's programme in Adult Education at Goldsmiths College. While I completed most of my units successfully, I faced an unfortunate setback when the course programme leader deferred one of my units. The leader unexpectedly instructed a lecturer to fail an assignment he had already passed, shocking me.

I felt upset about the covert racism that the programme leader and tutor displayed, and it was frustrating to have my passing grade turned into a fail. I met with the head of my faculty to address my concerns about my grade. He understood and promised to speak with my tutor about reinstating my passing grade. Unfortunately, he couldn't do anything about the grade given by the programme leader, who was accused of having racist biases. The head of the faculty agreed to supervise my dissertation, which passed and was even published in the educational journal Forum, Volume 42, Number 1.

Spring 2019. My son faced covert racism while pursuing his master's degree at the University of St Mark and St John in Plymouth in 2019. He was more scrutinised than his white peers despite providing all the necessary documents. He was also the only black student on his course, which followed a European curriculum. His associate professor, assigned as his dissertation supervisor, offered little constructive feedback and even ignored his emails.

My son faced various challenges with the Associated Professor during his time on the course. However, the situation worsened as his supervising tutor also began ignoring his emails and requesting appointments to visit his placement. As a result, he had to seek assistance from the programme leader to supervise his placement and address his concerns. As a result, my son's dissertation failed initially, but he eventually passed after it was referred to the academic board.

The challenges faced by Caribbeans living in the "Motherland" were brought to light by Jimmy Cliff. These struggles were overcome through sheer determination and the will to survive. Meanwhile, Dame Vera Lynn's song, "The White Cliff of Dover," became an instant hit. Unfortunately, Jimmy Cliff faced difficulties getting his song, "Many Rivers to Cross," to receive the same level of recognition. Our community has continually faced challenges for survival, dating back to the Middle Passage enslavement. Today, racism remains a persistent issue in areas such as employment, housing, education, the justice system, sports, and society in modern-day Britain.

Chapter 21

Britishness

The Windrush scandal commenced in 2017 after it became conspicuous that hundreds of Commonwealth citizens, many of whom emanated from the 'Windrush' generation, had been erroneously detained, deported, and denied legal rights. Victims of the Windrush scandal endured coerced maltreatment, a loss of employment, housing, and livelihoods, and were forcibly disunited from their families. They have often continued to have negative experiences due to hostile immigration policies.

At the time of my son's birth in 1986, I had full British citizenship; he, however, applied for his British passport, which should have been his legal entitlement. The Passport Office refused to grant him the passport, and the Home Office gave him two weeks' notice to leave the country to an unknown destination, leaving him stateless. He did eventually get a full British passport. However, the experience has left him traumatised and with trepidation when returning to the UK, as he is always stopped by UK Border Control Officers and questioned about his British status.

The Windrush scandal commenced in 2017 after it became apparent that hundreds of Commonwealth citizens, many of whom came from the 'Windrush' generation, had been wrongly detained, deported, and their legal rights to be in the UK were challenged. Victims of the Windrush scandal endured coerced maltreatment, a loss of employment, housing, and livelihoods, and were forcibly separated from their families. They have often perpetuated to have negative experiences as a result of hostile immigration policies.

The current covert racist practices of the Home Office and Border Force are a blatant breach of the Immigration Act 1973, which was subsequently replaced with the British Nationality Act 1981. The purpose of the law outlined who is eligible to live and should be liberated from being subjected to detainment or removal from the State. Nonetheless, the Act had illegally enforced restrictions on Commonwealth citizens with other citizens, ignoring the law that Commonwealth citizens, including the Caribbean, have never been economic 'migrants' workers, nor have they been non-Commonwealth nationals.

Victims of the merciless approach of ethnic cleansing have left many legal citizens traumatised, jobless, homeless, and forcibly disunited from their families. Many have committed suicide as a result of belligerent immigration policies.

There are unique standardised attributes between the Windrush scandal and the middle passage tragedy, where many enslaved individuals committed suicide because they preferred death over the prospect of being enslaved. In addition, many Caribbean citizens who were keen and answered the call to rebuild the "Motherland" were victims of racism, combativeness, alienation, and racial abuse on a monumental level and were treated worse than second-class citizens, with many of the host nations, we were aliens in the "Motherland."

Windrush victims endured non-stop negative experiences as a result of controversial immigration policies. The negative experience gained from the hateful "Motherland" has left many traumatise, alcohol and substance abuse, mental health, which are visible in family life, people lacking mental well-being and energy, not having the facility to interact with others effectively, Lack of confidence in the system that should provide relief and protection and facilities that would and encourage interaction with others linguistically, emotionally and socially.

Welcome to Mother land

The captive slaves from West Africa did not have a tradition of whipping children. They were young people who were aggressively enslaved, trafficked and subjected to physical whipping before being allocated to slave owners and while on plantations. Instead, traditional African parenting involved communication with children, meeting their emotional needs, living close to each other, telling folktales passed down from generation to generation, and setting clear boundaries for young people.

However, this traditional parenting style has become outdated, like their languages and religious practices were eradicated. If Middle Passage slaves were allowed to maintain their tribes, nationalities, or languages and continue their traditional methods, perhaps traditional African parenting could have been preserved. Unfortunately, these traditions were not valued by their slave owners, and the harsh style of punishment was perpetuated within the black community.

Chapter 22

Globalisation

The era of forced enslavement has ended, and black people are no longer governed by shackles or physical maltreatment. However, globalisation has introduced a new form of enslavement - dietary enslavement. As a result, Antiguans and other Caribbean islands have abandoned traditional foods in favour of quick meals owned by multinational companies.

This shift towards unhealthy options will undoubtedly impact the nation's health, as seen in Western societies. Fast food consumption is a ticking time bomb for children and adolescents, increasing their risk of obesity, cardiovascular disease, cholesterol, hypertension, mental fatigue, and lethargy. Globalisation has also affected indigenous Caribbean culture through trade liberalisation, technology, media, tourism, and migration.

The changes to our culture are evident throughout Antigua and the Caribbean, as external influences have increasingly become a part of our cultural identity. Before globalisation, the Caribbean diet followed many balanced nutrition guidelines the US Department of Agriculture set out. Our diet consisted of rich seafood, various fruits and vegetables, lean meats, and no refined products such as flour, grains, salt, and sugar. Antigua's history has led us to embrace foods from different cultures and make them our own, incorporating new ingredients in Antigua and other Caribbean regions.

The West Unhealthy options

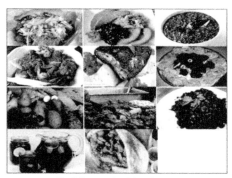

Caribbean Healthy Options

Chapter 23

The Aftermath

In many independent Caribbean islands, people are elated to have moved into the era of self-governance after being liberated from colonial rule. However, implementing neoliberal policies has made it difficult for small states to maintain their independence and has caused them to become financially enslaved. As a result, these states face challenges in diversifying their economies and remaining competitive within the guidelines of neoliberalism and globalisation.

Over the past fifty years, Western societies have pressured these small states, encouraging them to abandon their approach to self-governance and fiscal autonomy. As a result, local farmers are facing extinction due to these policies and are seeking access to European markets.

Globalisation has done more harm than good to our nation. Obstructions have continuously met all our efforts to pursue our independence. Working-class young people from socioeconomic backgrounds face high unemployment and poverty, and many have fallen victim to the drug culture without alternative resources. Foreign investors have acquired our lands to create businesses, leaving natives enslaved to foreign investors in our "independent" country.

As globalisation continues to grow, the ordinary working person, for example, street food vendors that provide local cuisines, are faced with fierce competition by foreign investors with sufficient financial resources systems in place that provides a cash-less society which in turn will impact the local entrepreneur whose main aim is to create a living to be self-sufficient. A local vendor would need the means to accept electronic payment for goods. Therefore, a cashless society would make it difficult for local entrepreneurs to compete.

It seems we're stuck in a cycle of oppression, first as enslaved individuals providing free labour for plantation owners and now as a population controlled financially. Despite this, we have little to celebrate, as Americanisation has overtaken our culture and daily lives. Many Antiguan homes now follow American customs with appliances like washing machines, dishwashers, microwaves, and electronic gadgets like laptops, mobile phones, and flat-screen TVs. Unfortunately, the language we inherited from our slave ancestors is becoming a thing of the past, and some frown upon wearing African attire. Adolescents may wear revealing clothing without issue, but older generations may disapprove.

Antigua's politicians were exposed to corruption following the end of colonial rule, which has become a part of everyday life on the island. Unfortunately, the withdrawal of colonial powers left Antigua with few resources, as they had been drained to build infrastructure in Europe. The corrupt system governing Antigua mainly depends on tourism, marketed as pristine beaches and beautiful weather. Many emerging countries, like Antigua, have deep-rooted issues from European colonialism.

Colonisers treated enslaved individuals and their descendants with cruelty and disrespect, leading to a belief that Britain and Europe were superior and sophisticated in ways that they were not. Poor leadership during colonial rule set a bad example for the country's future, leading to a corrupt system. While Antigua is no longer subject to enslavement and brutality, it is now under the oppressive tourism system. The industry impacts the lives of locals with low wages and mistreatment from visitors.

Descendants of the Windrush generation have experienced isolation, discrimination, and racism, with many still struggling from the traumas of separation and violence. Despite this, the Windrush generation has contributed immensely to the UK's arts, cuisine, and economy, though their sacrifices and contributions have not been adequately publicised. They are many negatives derived from the Windrush generations period that made the so-called "Motherland" a racist state.

Kelso Cochrane, a 32-year-old black man from Antigua, came to the "Motherland" to study law, but he was brutally murdered by a group of racist thugs on the streets of Ladbroke Grove in the Royal Borough of Kensington and Chelsea in May 1959. The killing of Kelso sparked the UK's first anti-racist riots in August-September 1959. The Police claimed that the murder of Kelso resulted from robbery, they burnt Kelso's clothes, and to date, the Metropolitan Police has not brought anyone before the Courts for the death of Cochrane.

The actions or inactions of the Metropolitan Police demonstrated that the Police and the Crown Prosecution Service were extemporary to put a white man on trial for the murder of a black man. Cochrane parents died without receiving justice for the murder of their son on the streets of the Motherland, and his extended family members have not had closure. He was, however, 'honoured' with a blue plaque at the venue where he was murdered. Notwithstanding, Stephen Lawrence was brutally murdered in the "Motherland" by racist thugs. The MacPherson inquiry in 1997 concluded that the

Metropolitan Police is institutionally racist. What has changed?

Kelso Cochrane 1926 – 17 May 1959

Conclusion

Leaving Antigua for London was unsettling for me. It felt like being uprooted from my familiar surroundings and planted in a foreign place, making me feel out of place. I spent much time adjusting to my new environment and dealing with the shock of being displaced. However, I was at an age where I could explore new experiences without losing touch with my roots. I didn't come to the UK because of the myth of Dick Whittington and his idea of London's streets being paved with gold.

Many Caribbean people were emotionally manipulated, deceived, and hurt by propaganda that promised a better life in the UK. However, upon their arrival, they discovered that the reality was far from what they had anticipated. This was particularly difficult for the Windrush generation, who left everything behind in the Caribbean expecting to find prosperity in the UK. Instead, they faced a nightmare that was beyond their worst fears. As a result, many of the Windrush generations suffered greatly and experienced profound humiliation, with some even resorting to sleeping in red telephone boxes. This experience also affected their children, who were expected to consider England their "Motherland" despite their difficulties.

I was shocked to discover that England lacked my home island's vibrant and exciting atmosphere in the sun. London, in particular, was a gloomy and dull place, but it still had an energy that made my heart race. Moving to this new place was a physical and emotional journey. I knew that to succeed, I would have to adapt to the local customs while still staying true to my Antiguan identity. I tried to learn Standard English, which meant sacrificing some of my ability to speak Antigua Creole with the proper accent, but I could still read and write in the language. The system was challenging, and I had to work hard to fit in, but I was determined to make it work.

Throughout the years, I have had the privilege of visiting my homeland twelve to fifteen times. Each trip has been a valuable learning experience that has made me more aware of my generation's sacrifices to shape Antigua into what it is today. Antigua has always provided me with comfort and familiarity, like a vibrant force within me. Being there, observing people, hearing their voices, and seeing how they do things similar to my own, gives me a feeling of control and simplicity. It's a peaceful retreat where I can appreciate the tranquillity and simplicity of life.

Black Windrush Caribbeans have deliberately declined while other races have advanced in infrastructure and opulence. Colonisation still plays an active part in the lives of Windrush Caribbeans. Windrush Caribbeans have been pigeon held while other races had a head start over us. In addition, slavery is still active today because Windrush Caribbeans were pigeons held by that era. Additionally, colonisation and slavery are responsible for racial inequality, discrimination, racism, and brokenness. They all have contributed to the lack of progress of the Windrush Caribbeans generation and their descendants.

The UK white power structure avoids talking about slavery; they would prefer not to engage and talk about the subject because the source of black-white racial inequality commenced from slavery. Additionally, the origin of police killings in the black community originated from slavery, as police killings are no different to the slaves' patrols, which were the commencement of policing.

The slaves' patrol was purported to keep the negroes on the plantation and to prevent them from running away. All the problems Windrush Caribbeans have encountered in the UK, Europe and America are derivatives of slavery and colonisation. The UK white power system does not surpass seventy years, the conversation is always fixated on what is occurring now, and it is never linked to its history because the UK white power system is reluctant to face up to the realisation that it's their system is the root cause of the Caribbean problem.

They focused heavily on knife and gun crime in black communities. They have predominantly overlooked the other races who used to kill each other. Killings in the non-black community have reduced over the years because those non-black races have gained economic stimulus packages. Consequently, Caribbeans have become marginalised and perpetuated being oppressed by the same system that enslaved us. It is paramount for Windrush Caribbeans to be aware of their political history, as the white oppressive system will continue to perceive the Windrush Caribbeans as the problem.

The Thatcher gentrification: The Yuppie era 1980s caused significant changes in black Windrush communities where black Windrush Caribbeans lived for decades in squalid conditions and deprivation to the point the Windrush Caribbean communities rose against their oppressors and demonstrated their dissatisfaction with being oppressed and took to the streets to let their voices heard. Significant works were set in motion throughout the Yuppie era to gentrify communities once occupied by Windrush generations and their descendants.

The gentrification projects forced the Windrush generations and descendants out of their communities, as they needed help to afford to rent or purchase properties they once lived in. The Windrush population did not own the means of wealth, and once again, many of them were victims of displacement. Many needed help to obtain bank loans or find employment equitably to meet the demands of rental charges or to buy. The government deliberately kept it that way with the full knowledge that the Windrush communities were not financially able to fight back because they did not own anything.

I am not deterred from the negative aspects of Windrush that descendants have encountered over the years, as oppressions are a part of the dominant system that was designed to keep black people as oppressed people. As a result, many offspring of the Windrush era were denied a curriculum; their rights to develop knowledge about their history were overlooked, and they were not educated about their forebears' contributions and where they hailed from.

Nevertheless, I remained grateful and appreciative of my forebears' undaunted contributions, and despite the odds, they added substantial financial value to an Empire that had enslaved them. Contrastingly, the regime and the Monarchy are resolute in not treating and appreciating Caribbeans by doing the right thing by apologising and making reparations for the wrongs they committed against us.

On the contrary, they have been limited promotion of the contributions made by the Windrush generations and their children from the White Gold era to the current day; they have almost become intangible because of the hostile society. The Windrush generations arrived in the UK mainly as Caribbean adults. Still, there is a variation between the adult generations and their children who were left behind and brought to the "Motherland"; I was one of them.

As an adolescent uprooted from my virgin soil, I witnessed terrifying happenings. I noticed people I assumed to be able to navigate my journey struggling with their navigation, which resulted from the realisation that they had also ended up somewhere foreign and out of the way. It was frightening to see or to be a victim where the adults wittingly or unwittingly; I think more of the latter that they became the child within their new place of abode.

For a long time, I tried to gain acceptance from my parents and fit in with them. I wanted to be included, understood, and approved of, but my mother made that difficult, if not impossible. I've had the privilege of travelling to many parts of Antigua. One of the most remarkable places I've visited is Hercules' Pillars, created from limestone. Seeing the waves crash against the pillars is breathtaking, but even more impressive is how the pillars stand firm against the forces of nature. Through my life experiences, I've learned to be resilient and not waste time seeking approval from others.

In 2014, I visited Antigua, intending to move back home. At the time, I was employed as an English specialist at the top college in London for eighteen years. The college was the ninth top college in the country and had received two awards from the late Queen for excellence in education. When I met with Michael Brown, the Minister for Education and the consistency member for All Saints West, he asked where in Antigua I was from and what my teaching methods were, but he used the wrong term for teaching curriculum.

Instead, he used the Greek Word "Pedagogy", which means "teaching methods". When I told him I was an English specialist, he abruptly said he couldn't help and showed me the door, telling me to take my CV. Leaving his office, I felt like a second-class citizen in my country of birth, where I had worked hard picking cotton at Pope's Head Estate and stacking cane to be conveyed to Gunthorpe's Sugar Factory to build Antigua.

Living in England opened my eyes to discrimination in the educational system and society. At eleven, I was classified as 'maladjusted' without consultation or support. Looking back, I realise that being a black male played a significant role in the mistreatment I faced in the UK. Discrimination followed me from primary school in the UK into adulthood, but I persevered despite the system's low expectations and my parent's expectations. While white peers received one-on-one support, I was denied a proper curriculum and left to struggle alone.

Fortunately, I found a supportive course tutor, Sylvia Stewart, at Brixton College, who helped me excel. I completed a challenging two-year certificate course awarded by the Central Council for Education and Training in Social Work. This programme helped me discover myself and ignited my passion to continue my education. Despite being written off by the headmaster of my former boarding school and their career advisor, who suggested I work in a factory or confectionery shop, I exceeded expectations and earned a Master's in Education. Discrimination may have been a part of my journey, but it did not define me or my potential.

Although I appreciate the shores of the UK, it's not my home. I was born and raised in Antigua, and its shores will always be home in my heart, but it's not where I currently reside. Antigua has changed, as have I, and that's okay.

My Antigua

Author's Biography

William Henry is an author from NewWinthropes Village, St. George, Antigua, who has advocated for justice and given a voice to the unheard for over forty-five years. He firmly believes that Caribbean Creole is a language with a structure similar to Standard English and deserves equal recognition.

In 1979, William obtained a certificate from the Central Council for Education and Social Work and worked in various Social Services Departments within Children and Family Services. Since 1992, he has taught Health and Social Care Core Subjects to Health Social Care practitioners at an FE College in Handsworth, Birmingham. His dedication to teaching helped him gradually work up to become a Course Tutor in Health and Social Care, despite initially being contracted for only two hours per week.

William has twenty-eight years of experience as an educator and spent eighteen years teaching the English Language at the top FE College in London. During his tenure, the college received two awards for Excellence in Education from the late Queen Elizabeth 2nd.

Feedback from a lesson observation carried out by an OFSTED Consultant:

General Comments by Observer- J Green:

- Very impressive attendance and punctuality are given weather conditions (16/18)

- Subject (obesity) interests students, and they show commitment in discussion allowing them to consider important issues around health, society, and equality. All students contributed to the group discussions; all felt they had something to offer.

- Clear focus on skills building: vocabulary, dictionary work, summarising and précis.

- Students work effectively in mixed-ability groups and support each other well; the teacher nurtured a very inclusive atmosphere in class.

- When talking to groups and individuals, students suggested that they felt well-supported and that their literacy skills were improving.

Good Practice to be shared with others and how this will be done (if appropriate):

- Attendance across key-skills classes variable, what methods does this teacher use to ensure good attendance even in adverse weather conditions? William can suggest some critical strategies to others (2013).

William was also accepted into membership as a Fellow with the Institute for Learning.

In 1996, William obtained a Certificate in Education from the University of Middlesex, and in 1999, he earned a Master of Arts in Education from Goldsmiths College. His dissertation, "The Use of Creole Alongside Standard English to Stimulate Students' Learning", was published in an Educational Journal called Forum, Volume 42 Number 1, Spring 2000. Additionally, in 2014, he received an Acentis Level 3 Diploma award in English for Literacy and Language.